REGENTS RENAISSANCE DRAMA SERIES

General Editor: Cyrus Hoy
Advisory Editor: G. E. Bentley

FRIAR BACON AND FRIAR BUNGAY

ROBERT GREENE

Friar Bacon and Friar Bungay

Edited by

DANIEL SELTZER

A BISON BOOK

UNIVERSITY OF NEBRASKA PRESS · LINCOLN

Library of Congress Catalog Card Number: 63–14697

MANUFACTURED IN THE UNITED STATES OF AMERICA

Regents Renaissance Drama Series

The purpose of the Regents Renaissance Drama Series is to provide soundly edited texts, in modern spelling, of the more significant plays of the Elizabethan, Jacobean, and Caroline theater. Each text in the series is based on a fresh collation of all sixteenth- and seventeenth-century editions. The textual notes, which appear above the line at the bottom of each page, record all substantive departures from the edition used as the copy-text. Variant substantive readings among sixteenth- and seventeenth-century editions are listed there as well. In cases where two or more of the old editions present widely divergent readings, a list of substantive variants in editions through the seventeenth century is given in an appendix. Editions after 1700 are referred to in the textual notes only when an emendation originating in some one of them is received into the text. Variants of accidentals (spelling, punctuation, capitalization) are not recorded in the notes. Contracted forms of characters' names are silently expanded in speech prefixes and stage directions, and, in the case of speech prefixes, are regularized. Additions to the stage directions of the copy-text are enclosed in brackets. Stage directions such as "within" or "aside" are enclosed in parentheses when they occur in the copy-text.

Spelling has been modernized along consciously conservative lines. "Murther" has become "murder," and "burthen," "burden," but within the limits of a modernized text, and with the following exceptions, the linguistic quality of the original has been carefully preserved. The variety of contracted forms (*'em, 'am, 'm, 'um, 'hem*) used in the drama of the period for the pronoun *them* are here regularly given as *'em,* and the alternation between *a'th'* and *o'th'* (for *on* or *of the*) is regularly reproduced as *o'th'*. The copy-text distinction between preterite endings in *-d* and *-ed* is preserved except where the elision of *e* occurs in the penultimate syllable; in such cases, the final syllable is contracted. Thus, where the old editions read "threat'ned," those of the present series read "threaten'd." Such contracted preterites in *-y'd* as "try'd," "cry'd," "deny'd," in the old editions, are here given as "tried," "cried," "denied."

Punctuation has been brought into accord with modern practices. The effort here has been to achieve a balance between the generally light pointing of the old editions, and a system of punctuation which, without overloading the text with exclamation marks, semicolons, and dashes, will make the often loosely flowing verse (and prose) of the original syntactically intelligible to the modern reader. Dashes are regularly used only to indicate interrupted speeches, or shifts of address within a single speech.

Explanatory notes, chiefly concerned with glossing obsolete words and phrases, are printed below the textual notes at the bottom of each page. References to stage directions in the notes follow the admirable system of the Revels editions, whereby stage directions are keyed, decimally, to the line of the text before or after which they occur. Thus, a note on 0.2 has reference to the second line of the stage direction at the beginning of the scene in question. A note on 115.1 has reference to the first line of the stage direction following line 115 of the text of the relevant scene.

CYRUS HOY

Vanderbilt University

Contents

Abbreviations

Baskervill	Charles Read Baskervill, Virgil B. Heltzel, and Arthur H. Nethercot, eds. *Elizabethan and Stuart Plays.* New York, 1934.
Collier	J. P. Collier, ed. *Dodsley's Old Plays,* Vol. VIII. London, 1825.
Collins	J. Churton Collins, ed. *The Plays and Poems of Robert Greene.* 2 vols. Oxford, 1905.
conj.	conjecture
Dickinson	Thomas H. Dickinson, ed. *Robert Greene.* The Mermaid Series. London, 1909.
Dyce	Alexander Dyce, ed. *The Dramatic Works of Robert Greene.* 2 vols. London, 1831.
Dyce 2	———, ed. *The Dramatic and Poetical Works of Robert Greene and George Peele.* London, 1861.
Gayley	Charles M. Gayley, ed. *Representative English Comedies.* New York, 1903.
Grosart	Alexander B. Grosart, ed. *The Life and Complete Works in Prose and Verse of Robert Greene,* Vol. XIII. 15 vols. London, 1881–1886.
MLN	*Modern Language Notes*
MLR	*Modern Language Review*
OED	*Oxford English Dictionary*
Q1	First Quarto of 1594
Q2	Second Quarto of 1630
Q3	Third Quarto of 1655
Schelling	Felix Schelling and M. W. Black, eds. *Typical Elizabethan Plays.* 2nd edn. New York, 1931.
S.D.	stage direction
SP	*Studies in Philology*
Ward	Adolphus W. Ward, ed. *Old English Drama: Select Plays.* Oxford, 1878.

Introduction

Friar Bacon was probably written in 1589, but because we lack definite evidence, its exact date must remain in doubt. Greene's *Alphonsus,* generally considered his first play, was written shortly after Marlowe's *Tamburlaine,* which dates from late 1587 or very early in the following year. Compared to *Alphonsus, Friar Bacon* is a more mature play in every respect, but how long before Greene's death (in September, 1592) it was written, is impossible to say. In July, 1588, he was incorporated Master of Arts at Oxford, and it is at least possible that about the time he received his degree, Greene decided to write a play about his new alma mater's great natural philosopher.

Several other relationships indicate a later, rather than an earlier date: (1) Former assumptions that *Friar Bacon* followed hard upon Marlowe's *Doctor Faustus,* and that the latter was written about 1587, have been seriously questioned.[1] If any indebtedness exists between the two playwrights, it is in fact much more likely that Marlowe, writing his play around 1592, actually borrowed here and there from Greene. (2) Between 1589 and 1591, in prefatory material to his *Farewell to Folly,* Greene wrote disparagingly of the anonymous author of *Fair Em,* a play whose theme partly resembles that of *Friar Bacon and Friar Bungay*; but even if we make the questionable assumption that Greene's attack was provoked by this resemblance, we have only proved that *Friar Bacon* dates earlier than 1591, since the relevant evidence admits of that late a date for *Fair Em.* (3) The general tone of patriotism in Greene's comedy may suggest a date after England's victory over the Spanish Armada, which was dispersed in July, 1588—the same month in which Greene received his Oxford M.A.—but, although such a spirit would be unlikely in a work written in the uneasy days before the Armada, the play contains no allusion specific enough to be admitted as absolute evidence.

[1] W. W. Greg, *Marlowe's Doctor Faustus 1606–1616: Parallel Texts* (Oxford, 1950), pp. 7–8, 10.

Edward's observation to Lacy that "next Friday is Saint James' [Day]" (i.134) is worth noting, because in 1589 Saint James's Day did indeed fall on a Friday. Although Elizabethan playwrights did not always use the calendar of the current year for such purposes, the possibility rings true that, in this case, Greene did so.[2] In all events, the period 1589–1590 remains the most plausible guess for the date of the play. The first mention of it, an entry in the diary of Philip Henslowe for February 19, 1592, does not mark it as a new play, and it is likely that its first performances took place soon after its completion.

Henslowe notes in this entry that he received "at fryer bacvne the 19 of febrary satterdaye . . . xvij^{s} iij^{d}," and later records that *Friar Bacon* was produced three more times during the year, and three times again in January, 1593.[3] All seven performances were by Lord Strange's Men at the Rose Theatre. In April, 1594, the play was revived in two performances by the Queen's Men and Sussex's Men, playing jointly at the Rose (Henslowe, I, 17), and in May of that year it was entered in the Stationers' Register and subsequently printed. Greene's name appears on the title page of this quarto, and there is no reason to question his authorship. The title page also offers the play "As it was plaid by her Maiesties seruants," but the records of its ownership by the Queen's Men are very much in doubt. This company, declining rapidly in importance as early as 1589, had established joint performance with Sussex's Men in 1591. Although they may have owned Greene's play originally, it is possible that around 1591 *Friar Bacon* passed into the hands of the actor Edward Alleyn, and thence to Henslowe and Strange's Men for the performances noted above.

To judge from Henslowe's receipts, the play was a definite success. He still owned it in 1602, two years after the Fortune was built, for he records the Admiral's Men's commission "vnto m^{r} mydelton for a prologe & a epeloge for the playe of bacon for the corte" (Henslowe, I, 172), for which the playwright received five shillings. (These pieces by Middleton are not known today.) The 1630 quarto states on its title page that *Friar Bacon* is printed "As it was lately plaied by the Prince *Palatine* his Seruants." This company followed Prince Henry's in succeeding the Admiral's;

[2] See F. G. Fleay, *A Biographical Chronicle of the English Drama 1559–1642* (London, 1891), I, 264–265.

[3] W. W. Greg, ed., *Henslowe's Diary* (London, 1904), I, 13–16.

evidently the play remained in the hands of the Admiral's Men after such court performances as that recorded in 1602 by Henslowe, and, although Sir Henry Herbert makes no mention of it in the Revels accounts between 1623 and 1673, we may assume that it was acted occasionally during the reigns of James and Charles I.

There are three early editions of *Friar Bacon and Friar Bungay,* but only the first of these, the rare quarto of 1594, has any textual value. The quarto of 1630 was printed from the first, introducing some normalization of spelling and, occasionally, of grammar, correcting some printer's errors but adding many more, and reproducing some as they stood. The quarto of 1655 was printed mainly if not entirely from that of 1630. No important corrections appear in either of the later editions, and they are clearly derivative of the first. The 1594 quarto, then, must be regarded as the substantive text of the play. It survives in only four known copies, none of them bibliographically complete, although the copy discovered in 1936 in the library of Corpus Christi College, Oxford, is the most perfect. Except for one unimportant press variant, it is the best exemplar of the substantive text, and therefore has been used as the control-text of this edition. The present text has been conservatively modernized, but is based upon the 1594 quarto for all readings except for clear press mistakes and equally clear textual corruption. All important corrections and emendations are recorded in the notes. Unless emendation seemed absolutely necessary, the readings of the 1594 quarto have been retained.

The play is one of the more interesting specimens of Elizabethan drama very likely printed from theatrical copy. The stage direction in which Miles is instructed to "sit down and knock [his] head" (xi.49.1) is almost certainly a playhouse addition, and since it is not the sort of instruction which would have been of any use to the prompter, may be an example of direction in rehearsal. Other stage directions which indicate properties (xi.0.1–3), stage business (iii.35.1, xi.38), costume disguise (iii.0.1–3, v.0.1–2), mood (i.0.1), or offstage effects (xi.52.1), could be either authorial or theatrical in origin, but an overall impression suggests that the printer did have at his disposal copy which had been used by actors.

The materials from which Greene constructed *Friar Bacon* fall into two categories. First, there is a body of specific source material drawn from printed books and legends of great antiquity. Then, there are two shaping influences of unspecific origin—responsible not only for this play, but, in the one case, for a formalized presentation in Elizabethan writing of constancy in women, and, in the other, for a complicated attitude toward the practice of magic. The first of these is a literary influence; the second, harder to categorize, was diffuse and ill-defined.

Greene's major printed source was an anonymous prose romance, probably dating from the middle of the sixteenth century,[4] but surviving today in no copy earlier than an edition of 1627. Its inviting title reads, in full, *The Famous Historie of Fryer Bacon. Containing the wonderfull things that he did in his Life: Also the manner of his Death; With the Liues and Deaths of the two Conjurers* Bungye *and* Vandermast, *Very pleasant and delightfull to be read.* There is some indication that Greene took one or two names of his noblemen from Holinshed's *Chronicles* for the year 1264, and, possibly, other details and minor associations from works by John Bale, John Foxe, Johannes Nauclerus, and Giordano Bruno. He was apparently familiar as well with the medieval romance tradition of the benevolent (and occasionally heroic) sorcerer—the magician at once learned and patriotic, such as Merlin, in some of the Arthurian stories, or Oberon, in *Huon of Bordeaux*.[5] The similarities between such magicians and Bacon, however, tell us more about the hero of the prose romance than the sorcerer of Greene's play, for in his interesting use of *The Famous Historie,* the playwright went to some pains to limit the benevolence of the hero he found there. He made four major changes in the plot material of the prose romance: (1) All specific references to Bacon as a churchman are eliminated. (2) Greene omitted as well many of Bacon's patriotic intentions found throughout the action of *The Famous Historie,* but emphasized both these and generally religious allusions at the very end of the

[4] See W. F. McNeir, "Traditional Elements in the Character of Greene's *Friar Bacon,*" *SP,* XLV (1948), 172–179. The most readily available modern edition of the source (although it is not printed with complete accuracy) is included in W. J. Thoms, ed., *Early English Prose Romances* (London, n.d. [1907]).

[5] See McNeir, "Traditional Elements"; P. Z. Round, "Greene's Materials for *Friar Bacon and Friar Bungay,*" *MLR,* XXI (1926), 19–23; J. D. McCallum, "Greene's *Friar Bacon and Friar Bungay,*" *MLN,* XXXV (1920), 212–217.

play. (3) In the source, Bacon is careful to tell the King that his wonderful achievements are the results of science, not magic; in the play, the emphasis on black magic is increased at every opportunity. (4) Most important, Greene rearranged the character relationships in that portion of the romance in which Friar Bacon sides with an "Oxfordshire Gentleman" (Lacy) in his love for a "faire Mayde" (Margaret), desired as well by a rich knight (Edward). In the source, the seducing knight pays Bungay (who is said to be "couetous") to "hamper up the match"; the gentleman comes to Bacon for help, which is as effective as it is astonishing, and the girl marries her true lover—with Bungay struck dumb by Bacon's magic (a detail Greene retained). In his play, Greene reversed the roles of the two friars. In this, as in the other source revisions, he clearly was trying to equate his wizard-hero, for the major portion of the action, to that danger which, in most forms of tragicomedy, will threaten and test the felicity of true love. There is no denying, of course, that the tone of the play remains light; even the satire of academicians is not cynical, but touched with comic tomfoolery. Nevertheless, one returns with some uneasiness to the terminology and fervor of Bacon's repentance, to the unmistakable aims of Prince Edward in regard to Margaret, and to those changes which Greene made in the source story, in which he obviously placed the magician, for a time, on the side of villainy.

Evidence pertaining to Renaissance opinion of the occult sciences is so often contradictory that a general viewpoint is impossible to isolate. The orthodox view condemned such studies as unchristian, although in the drama there seem to be varying degrees of condemnation of their practice, ranging from the most severe (as in Marlowe's *Faustus*) to passing references indicative of little concern. It would not do to state categorically that every Elizabethan believed in the powers of magic, but it would be equally false to make a case for scientific skepticism as the typical state of mind. That Greene placed his wizard on the side of wrong was in keeping with the popular opinion of the historical Roger Bacon, who was considered a demonologist and a sorcerer—in spite of occasional protests by Elizabethan scientists. Whatever his personal views may have been, there can be little doubt that when Greene chose the subject matter of sorcery for presentation upon the popular stage, his moral orientation and vocabulary were those, by and large, of his popular audience, whose opinion was that men of learning who meddled with the devil could not—by definition—acknowledge the infinite power of the Christian God. Therefore, in their mysterious and prideful abilities, such scholars ran the risk of damnation. Friar Bacon's speech of repentance (xiii.85–108) fully illustrates this belief, especially in the admission that his conjuring of spirits and devils was aimed at equaling the efficacy of God.

Bacon's most wonderful properties in the play are his brazen head and his magical glass. Greene's treatment of the head is derived more or less directly from *The Famous Historie*. That of the glass, however, is in terms of popular lore, even though the source insists that Bacon's exploits, no matter how marvelous, were entirely explicable and "nothing Magicall." This portion of the source is, in fact, a rambling paraphrase of Chapters IV and V of the real Roger Bacon's treatise, *De nullitate magiae*, a work of detailed technology which attempts to disprove the necessity of magic in working such wonders. Greene could not have been ignorant of contemporary interest in and experimentation with the telescope, but apparently he chose to ignore any technical explanation of these instruments (such explanations were not rare), along with their usual insistence that their wonders were accomplished through natural means. Even if he ever became interested in the sciences of visual phenomena, Greene's postgraduate degrees are hardly relevant there; the narrative material used in *Friar Bacon* has very little to do with scientific treatises, and the form of the play would lack clarity if it did. By making perfectly sure that Bacon's glass appeared in the popular and not the learned tradition—by carefully eschewing the source's explanation that Bacon's wonders were "nothing Magicall"—the glass in the play could be made an instrument of harmful sorcery, and, through its use, a real threat to the happiness of the lovers.

Even though the seriousness of Bacon's art is eventually lightened through the comic decorum of the play, it is important to remember its basically dangerous significance, and not to confuse it with so-called "white" magic, or theurgy. During the late Middle Ages and the Renaissance, there was evidently thought to be a kind of magic which could be thoroughly potent in its contact with spirits and yet not damnable; but repeated qualifications and outright protests by popular writers point to the truth of the matter: there could be no sorcery which was not to some degree suspect. Any power which could call up spirits—be they neoplatonic "daemons" or necromantic "demons"—could not claim the assistance of God, and must, therefore, receive the aid of the devil. No doubt many sincere masters of religio-science (such as the most poignantly misunderstood eccentric of Elizabeth's reign, Dr. John Dee) believed they were seeking "the fruit and end of Natural Philosophy, being vsed as christen men ought to vse it."[6] But it was an easy step from their yearning to understand things past ordinary perception—the goal, for example, of the Friar Bacon in the anonymous play, *John of Bordeaux* (very likely by Greene)—to the inordinate desire for knowledge which causes Faustus (the legendary magician as well as Marlowe's hero) to call upon the powers of hell. Knowledge of natural philosophy should be used to gain heaven. This is essentially the goal of Prospero's "Art" in *The Tempest*; but ultimately even this science must be abjured, and the book drowned. In the popular tradition the most sanctimonious explanation for any sort of conjuring was met with tongue in cheek. "Halfe witches are they," exclaimed Thomas Nashe, "that pretending anie Religion, meddle halfe with God, and halfe with the diuell. Medling with the diuell I call it, when ceremonies are obserued which haue no ground from Diuinitie." Furthermore, "the greatest and notablest heathen sorcerers that euer were, in all their hellish adiurations, vsed the name of the one true and euer-liuing God: but such a number of damned potestates they ioined with him, that it might seeme the starres had darkned the sunne."[7]

It would not have been surprising to an Elizabethan audience that Bacon's "medling with the diuell" should cause death—as in that remarkable scene in which two students witness the fatal duel of their fathers, and then kill each other—nor that it would be allied with lust. Prince Edward's intentions regarding Margaret, until his change of heart, amount to nothing less than rape (his early comparison of himself to Tarquin and of Margaret to Lucrece is apt), and although there are magicians in the literature

[6] John Dee, *A necessary Advertizement*, ed. James Crossley, Publications of the Chetham Society No. 24 (Manchester, 1851), pp. 62–63; and see P. H. Kocher, *Science and Religion in Elizabethan England* (San Marino, 1953), p. 135; F. R. Johnson, *Astronomical Thought in Renaissance England* (Baltimore, 1937), pp. 80, 177–178; John Dee, *The Elements of Geometrie of* [*Euclid*] . . . (London, 1570), Sigs. Ai^{v}–Aii.

[7] "Terrors of the Night," *Works of Thomas Nashe*, ed. R. B. McKerrow; corr. and suppl. by F. P. Wilson (Oxford, 1958), I, 358–359.

of romance who bring about happy marriages, Bacon's use of knowledge is directed at first to other ends. It was an accepted convention in this literature that only firm chastity could withstand the power of lust allied with sorcery, and Edward knows that with Margaret it is "marriage or no market" (i.121)—the coldly casual "market" undercutting the Prince's Petrarchan blazons in her praise. The Bacon of *John of Bordeaux* may exclaim angrily, "Was magic/ Therefore meant to maintain wrong, to force/ Chaste ladies yield to foolish lust?"—but the hero-wizard of *Friar Bacon and Friar Bungay* never so much as reprimands the prince, and agrees willingly to "strain out [his] magic spells" (v.100). Although real or possible disaster seems to alternate in this play with comic horseplay, with the result that Bacon's demonology is funny almost as often as it is dangerous, there is no doubt that his eleventh-hour repentance is required by his earlier misdeeds.

In constructing the play, it was necessary for Greene to place such an emphasis on Bacon's magic. Without it, the order which triumphs in the last scene, in marriage and in the state, would triumph untested. Such testing—a device roughly equivalent to the quests of medieval romances—was essential to the form of tragicomedy. The happiness threatened by sorcery in *Friar Bacon* is that of love—love as the major antidote for the vagaries of fortune, as the primary power for rejuvenation in nature. In this sort of comedy, the wedding march merges with the ceremonial march of kings and princes who rule happy and prosperous countries; human love, once tested, is instrumental in effecting such order. All of Greene's known plays (and a few others very likely by him) end with a comic celebration of natural order in the marriage, reunion, or reconciliation of lovers and, simultaneously, in the establishment of felicity in the state. Greene's careful structuring of *Friar Bacon* brings all the characters, at some point, under the wholesome influence of Margaret of Fressingfield, just as, at one juncture or another, they come in contact with Bacon. The demonologist's actions in the story endanger and delay the consummation of virtuous love, while Margaret's represent the felicity which is to win through. Her character derives partly from the source story, but mainly from the literary tradition behind many of Greene's ladies—that of virtuous women who are beautiful, constant, and redemptive. She is a combination of two ordinarily related *personae* in the literature of medieval and

Renaissance romance, the lady of nobility who lives in lowly surroundings and the figure of Patient Griselda. Edward is instructed by her constancy, and, his natural courtly virtue triumphing, turns from her to his Spanish princess; Margaret's own beauties and virtues, although lowly, are carefully described in courtly terms (e.g., i.50–61 and 72–86). This mixed vocabulary, full of homely and classical imagery, makes "Suffolk's fair Helen" (x.35) as explicitly regal as she is explicitly humble, and tells us, in effect, that Lacy is not *really* in love below his station after all.

The Griselda figure was always used to express steadfastness so extreme as to be almost miraculous. Attracted throughout his literary career to the subject matter of lowly nobility, Greene would have realized that the story of Patient Griselda provided motivation for a number of plot-lines, and that it contained great potential for discussion of ethical problems connected with ideals of constancy. More important, the basic story of Griselda (its roots firmly embedded in folklore long before Boccaccio, Petrarch, and Chaucer wrote their versions of the tale[8]), stripped of any sophistication and speaking purely in dramatic terms, is a story in which the action is specifically a test. The remarkable response of the lady to her betrayal is purely exemplary, and not psychologically motivated. It is a story in which moral significance cannot be separated from plot. The test in *Friar Bacon* begins with Edward's solicitation of Margaret, but reaches its climax in Lacy's letter to her. This letter is introduced with no warning, no preliminary hint in any earlier scene. No realistic motivation would have been necessary, for Greene's audiences would have found the logical emphasis where in fact it occurs, in Margaret's response. Unlike those Elizabethan and Jacobean plays in which the testing of the Griselda figure is motivated by a cynically realistic view of the world (usually suggested to the husband by a vice figure, such as Politic Persuasion in Phillip's *Patient Grissell,* or, for that matter, Iago, in *Othello*), the testing of fidelity in the pastoral tragicomedy simply reinforces the natural nobility of the lady of low station—whether she is actually a country girl or a real princess disguised as a shepherdess. The testing is therefore a hyperbolic restatement of a character already perceived by the audience, and although suspense is not removed by making the threat to constancy too

[8] See W. A. Cate, "The Problem of the Origin of the Griselda Story," *SP*, XXIX (1932), 389–405.

feeble, the test and its results, on all levels of action, prove the lady worthy of noble love.

Greene's Margaret is not identical in all respects to the traditional figure of Griselda, but because the more important resemblances are preserved, the moral values of the original become part of the texture of the play. In *Friar Bacon,* the dangers to the heroine are, if anything, more severe than the traditional sorrows of the story; nor have we been assured at the beginning of the play (as was the audience of Greene's *Alphonsus)* that the plot will unfold "in the manner of a comedy," thus vitiating the dramatic power opposing the forces of good. In what is probably his last play, *James IV,* Greene places his Griselda-heroine, Dorothea, in even greater danger, and brings the action very close to tragedy; in *Friar Bacon,* it is interesting to observe his efforts to maintain suspense and a comic decorum simultaneously, by humanizing the traditional emblem behind his heroine and by undercutting Bacon's magic with occasional slapstick humor.

It is ordinarily observed that Margaret is the first realistic heroine in Elizabethan drama, anticipating Rosalind, Portia, and Viola. This is not entirely true, for Margaret's apparent liveliness owes as much to the theatrical situations which surround her as to a fully articulated character of her own. Greene makes some effort to give his other country "clowns" an approximation of the diction of common life (e.g., iii.1–4, 56–59; x.63), but Margaret speaks by the book; her speech sounds, for the most part, as Greg observed, as though she had spent her girlhood reading Greene's courtly prose romances. On the other hand, her response to the conventional situations of the Griselda story can be humanly complex. When the husband in the original tale tells his wife that another woman will replace her, she humbly takes her leave and returns home to her father. This uncomplicated response is retained, for example, in the Griselda plays of Phillips and Dekker (and cf. *Othello,* III.iv.148–154). When Lacy's letter arrives, Margaret, like the archetype, prays for his happiness (x.168–169), but she is allowed as well a hint of reproach (x.150–152). Furthermore, Greene proceeds to represent her constancy in terms occasionally so hyperbolic as to be amusing: she will denounce the world entirely and enter a nunnery. The decision, of course, is nothing if not virtuous, but Greene's attitude, although it is never harshly satiric, suggests that such a vow may also be laughable. Through the slightly bombastic lines of Margaret's resolution (x.158–162;

xiv.8–26, 29–38), Greene gently implies that to become a nun would be folly, and his treatment of the character becomes delightfully clear as she builds to peroration: "But even to that, as to the rest, farewell"—for here, with the same superb sense of stage timing which had brought Bacon on at the height of Vandermast's victory, is the welcome stage direction: "*Enter* Lacy, Warren, Ermsby, *booted and spurred.*" There is no doubt as to Margaret's choice, between "God or Lord Lacy." In this episode Greene adds to an emblem the reassuring dimensions of flesh and blood. The scene reveals, nevertheless, how conscious Greene has been of the literary posture which now may be slightly relaxed.

Although the felicity of love is threatened by Bacon's magic, the playwright's light touch in dealing with the materials of academic sorcery mitigates its awesomeness. Any spectator or reader of *Friar Bacon* will observe that Greene has placed his hero just to one side of complete responsibility for evil action. The texture of the play, which is comic, modifies the formal mold of this character, and although on the printed page the comic horseplay and the formal mold do not always blend, this would not be disturbing—nor most of the time even noticeable—during performance. For example, the atmosphere at the end of Scene vi, in which Margaret and Lacy watch Bungay carried off by one of Bacon's devils, is one of levity, not fearsome seriousness. In Scene ii, when Bacon conjures "*per omnes deos infernales,*" a greasy kitchen wench appears, carrying a shoulder of mutton. Miles's warning to the assembled scholars (ii.114) tells us that they are showing their fright; but no doubt Greene's audiences laughed at this point in much the same way we laugh at a modern comedian's reaction to the skeleton in a closet. There is no doubt about the skeleton: it is real and meaningful. But there is relief in observing its discovery by someone else—especially if his reaction in fear is an exaggerated image of ours. Just as surely as the skeleton implies death, and is frightening, Bacon's contract with hell is explicit and would have been frightening; similarly, the laughter it elicited would have been in part defensive.

The figure of the over-proud magician contained as much potential for comedy as for tragedy. Greene was typical of his age not only in holding demonology wicked, but in connecting its vanity with the pride of scholars ill at ease in any world save one of their making. That vanity, as any other, could be productive of humor. Our cue is Miles's allusion to Barclay's famous Ship, which he will conjure from Oxford, he says, "with colleges and schools full loaden with fools" (vii.86). This ship, the tipsy clown has warned the doctors, will "carry away the Niniversity with a fair wind to the Bankside in Southwark" (vii.72–73). Whatever his pride in his own degrees, Greene seems to have planned his treatment of Oxford scholars—and certainly of Oxford's great doctor of natural philosophy—in the same spirit. Such a cunning philosopher, Greene wrote elsewhere, "by long staring at the stars forgets the globe at his feet," and, after reviewing the dusty researches of such men, concluded that their endeavors could become "a tickling humour of selfe loue, that may bring scollers within the compasse of pride. . . ."[9] A Christian distrust of powers obtained from devils is the reason why Bacon's magic can become the danger required by the tragicomic plot, but this danger is in turn mitigated by the comedy inherent in a wizard's folly; a sorcerer is funny if he is also an over-proud scholar. In this, Greene's approach is not unlike Folly's remarks on the scientists, in Erasmus's great mock encomium: "They assign causes for lightning, winds, eclipses, and other inexplicable things, never hesitating a whit, as if they were privy to the secrets of nature, artificer of things, or as if they visited us fresh from the council of the gods."[10] To gloss these words from *The Praise of Folly*, one might add Greene's own observation, in his *Never Too Late,* that "[scholars'] aphorisms of art, are dissolued with this definit period *Omnia sub sole vanitas*" (VIII, 16).

At the end of the play, Bacon begins his prognostication of political stability and fruitful love by repenting once more "the follies of [his] youth,/ That magic's secret mysteries misled" (xvi.36–37). When he repents, the art which had taught him prophetic powers becomes implicitly virtuous, for his learning—now similar to Prospero's—has become an ordered control of nature born of Christian contemplation. Paralleling Bacon's assumption of the proper use of knowledge is Edward's return, in Scene viii, to the true honor of a prince, achieved when he blesses the marriage of Margaret and Lacy. The complex plots of *Friar Bacon,*

[9] "Farewell to Folly," *The Life and Complete Works in Prose and Verse of Robert Greene,* ed. A. B. Grosart (London, 1881–1886), IX, 241, 250.

[10] Desiderius Erasmus, *The Praise of Folly,* trans. H. H. Hudson (Princeton, 1941), pp. 76–77 (Section 27). See also Sections 25, on Grammarians, and 28, on Theologians.

taken as a whole, are an extended proof of human ability to redeem folly, each story-line reinforcing the main theme.

Ultimately, the play celebrates natural order. The carefully planned structure which accomplishes this was a great advance in the technique of Tudor drama, and is typical of stagecraft which taught "the only Shake-scene in a country" more about the making of plays than he learned from any other predecessor. Whatever Greene may have been like during the last unhappy and ungenerous months before his death, there is a generosity of spirit in *Friar Bacon* which again and again reminds us of Shakespeare. The rugged, frequently eloquent verse often rings of the English countryside—as it does, for example, when Serlsby promises Margaret his "forty kine with fair and burnish'd heads,/ With strouting dugs that paggle to the ground" (x.62–63)—and the play as a whole implies that human beings are created with a natural propensity for good. In *Friar Bacon,* the courtly virtues of magnanimity and gentleness are seen as natural human resources, and are celebrated in the cumulative effect of the plot. To delight in such virtues may be said to reveal them in the playwright himself, and since everything we know about Greene's life is so generally sordid, it is only fair to point out that this play, in eschewing misanthropy and in praising humanity, is typical of his best writing for the Elizabethan stage.

DANIEL SELTZER

Harvard University

FRIAR BACON AND FRIAR BUNGAY

[Characters of the Play

KING HENRY THE THIRD
EDWARD, PRINCE OF WALES, *his son*
EMPEROR OF GERMANY
KING OF CASTILE
DUKE OF SAXONY
LACY, *Earl of Lincoln* } *Edward's friends*
WARREN, *Earl of Sussex* } *Edward's friends*
ERMSBY, *a Gentleman* } *Edward's friends*
RAFE SIMNELL, *the King's fool*
FRIAR BACON
MILES, *his poor scholar*
FRIAR BUNGAY
JACQUES VANDERMAST, *a German magician*
BURDEN } *Oxford doctors*
MASON } *Oxford doctors*
CLEMENT } *Oxford doctors*
LAMBERT } *Country squires*
SERLSBY } *Country squires*
TWO SCHOLARS, *their sons*
THE KEEPER OF FRESSINGFIELD
HIS FRIEND
THOMAS } *Rustics*
RICHARD } *Rustics*
A CONSTABLE
A POST, *serving Lacy*

LORDS, GENTLEMEN, SERVANTS, *attending King Henry's court*
COUNTRY CLOWNS *at Harleston Fair*

ELEANOR, *daughter to the King of Castile*
MARGARET, *the Keeper's daughter, called the Fair Maid of Fressingfield*
JOAN, *a country wench*
HOSTESS OF THE BELL, *at Henley*

TWO DEVILS
THE VOICE OF BACON'S BRAZEN HEAD
A SPIRIT IN THE SHAPE OF HERCULES]

The Honorable History of Friar Bacon and Friar Bungay

[i]

Enter [Prince Edward], *malcontented; with* Lacy, Earl of Lincoln; John Warren, Earl of Sussex; *and* Ermsby, Gentleman; Rafe Simnell, *the King's fool;* [*other lords and gentlemen*].

LACY.

Why looks my lord like to a troubled sky
When heaven's bright shine is shadowed with a fog?
Alate we ran the deer, and through the lawns
Stripp'd with our nags the lofty frolic bucks
That scudded 'fore the teasers like the wind.
Ne'er was the deer of merry Fressingfield
So lustily pull'd down by jolly mates,
Nor shar'd the farmers such fat venison,
So frankly dealt, this hundred years before;
Nor have I seen my lord more frolic in the chase,
And now chang'd to a melancholy dump.

0.1. *Prince Edward*] *Edward the first Q1–3.*

0.1–3. The entrance probably would have been accompanied by stage sounds representing the hunt.

0.1. *malcontented*] melancholy; a formalized state of mind in Elizabethan acting, probably represented in costuming and posture.

4. *Stripp'd*] out-stripped.

4. *frolic*] merry, joyous.

5. *teasers*] dogs trained to chase the game, as opposed to those used to pull it down.

6. *Fressingfield*] a village in Suffolk; with Harleston and Framlingham, almost directly south of Norwich.

9. *frankly dealt*] freely given.

11. *dump*] sadness, reverie, confusion.

WARREN.

After the Prince got to the keeper's lodge
And had been jocund in the house a while,
Tossing of ale and milk in country cans,
Whether it was the country's sweet content,
Or else the bonny damsel fill'd us drink,
That seem'd so stately in her stammel red,
Or that a qualm did cross his stomach then,
But straight he fell into his passions.

ERMSBY.

Sirrah Rafe, what say you to your master,
Shall he thus all amort live malcontent?

RAFE.

Hearest thou, Ned? Nay, look if he will speak to me.

EDWARD.

What say'st thou to me, fool?

RAFE.

I prithee tell me, Ned, art thou in love with the keeper's daughter?

EDWARD.

How if I be, what then?

RAFE.

Why then, sirrah, I'll teach thee how to deceive love.

EDWARD.

How, Rafe?

RAFE.

Marry, sirrah Ned, thou shalt put on my cap and my coat and my dagger, and I will put on thy clothes and thy sword, and so thou shalt be my fool.

EDWARD.

And what of this?

---

16. *fill'd*] who filled.
17. *stammel*] coarse woolen cloth, usually red.
21. *all amort*] dejected (from Fr. *à la mort*).
29–30. *cap . . . dagger*] the professional jester's properties, including the cockscomb cap and slapstick dagger of lath, the latter frequently carried by the Vice in morality plays.

RAFE.

Why, so thou shalt beguile Love, for Love is such a proud scab that he will never meddle with fools nor children. Is not Rafe's counsel good, Ned?

EDWARD.

Tell me, Ned Lacy, didst thou mark the maid,
How lively in her country weeds she look'd?
A bonnier wench all Suffolk cannot yield.
All Suffolk! Nay, all England holds none such.

RAFE.

Sirrah Will Ermsby, Ned is deceived.

ERMSBY

Why, Rafe?

RAFE.

He says all England hath no such, and I say, and I'll stand to it, there is one better in Warwickshire.

WARREN.

How provest thou that, Rafe?

RAFE.

Why, is not the Abbot a learned man and hath read many books, and thinkest thou he hath not more learning than thou to choose a bonny wench? Yes, I warrant thee, by his whole grammar.

ERMSBY.

A good reason, Rafe.

EDWARD.

I tell thee, Lacy, that her sparkling eyes
Do lighten forth sweet love's alluring fire;
And in her tresses she doth fold the looks
Of such as gaze upon her golden hair;

47–48. I warrant thee] *Q1*; warrant I thee *Q2–3*.

---

33. *beguile*] trick.
34. *scab*] merry wag, roaring boy.
37. *lively*] gay, animated.
37. *weeds*] garments.
45–48. *Abbot . . . grammar*] i.e., "the Abbot is lecherous in direct proportion to his learning, which is greater, by the whole grammar, than yours."

Her bashful white mix'd with the morning's red
Luna doth boast upon her lovely cheeks;
Her front is beauty's table, where she paints
The glories of her gorgeous excellence;
Her teeth are shelves of precious margarites
Richly enclosed with ruddy coral cleeves.
Tush, Lacy, she is beauty's over-match,
If thou survey'st her curious imagery.

LACY.
I grant, my lord, the damsel is as fair
As simple Suffolk's homely towns can yield;
But in the court be quainter dames than she,
Whose faces are enrich'd with honor's taint,
Whose beauties stand upon the stage of fame
And vaunt their trophies in the courts of Love.

EDWARD.
Ah, Ned, but hadst thou watch'd her as myself,
And seen the secret beauties of the maid,
Their courtly coyness were but foolery.

ERMSBY.
Why, how watch'd you her, my lord?

EDWARD.
When as she swept like Venus through the house,
And in her shape fast folded up my thoughts,
Into the milkhouse went I with the maid,

61. survey'st] *Q1–2*; surpast *Q3*.

---

54. *bashful*] modest.
54. *white . . . red*] the traditionally praised colors of the Petrarchan blazons.
56. *front*] forehead, or whole countenance.
56. *table*] a panel for painting. 56. *she*] i.e., personified Beauty.
58. *margarites*] pearls, probably with a play on the heroine's name.
59. *cleeves*] cliffs. 61. *curious imagery*] exquisite features.
63. *homely*] humble. 64. *quainter*] more rare.
65. *taint*] hue, tint.
67. *courts of Love*] allusion to chivalric tribunals in which questions of gallantry were decided; cf. viii.85.
68. *as myself*] as I did. 69. *secret*] less obvious.
70. *foolery*] flirtation.
72. *When as*] when.

And there amongst the cream bowls she did shine
As Pallas 'mongst her princely huswifery.
She turn'd her smock over her lily arms
And dived them into milk to run her cheese;
But, whiter than the milk, her crystal skin,
Checked with lines of azure, made her blush,
That art or nature durst bring for compare.
Ermsby, if thou hadst seen as I did note it well,
How beauty play'd the huswife, how this girl,
Like Lucrece, laid her fingers to the work,
Thou wouldest with Tarquin hazard Rome and all
To win the lovely maid of Fressingfield.

RAFE.

Sirrah Ned, wouldst fain have her?

EDWARD.

Ay, Rafe.

RAFE.

Why, Ned, I have laid the plot in my head thou shalt have her already.

EDWARD.

I'll give thee a new coat, and learn me that.

RAFE.

Why, sirrah Ned, we'll ride to Oxford to Friar Bacon. Oh, he is a brave scholar, sirrah; they say he is a brave nigromancer, that he can make women of devils, and he can juggle cats into costermongers.

EDWARD.

And how then, Rafe?

RAFE.

Marry, sirrah, thou shalt go to him, and because thy father Harry shall not miss thee, he shall turn me into

---

76. *Pallas . . . huswifery*] Pallas Athene was among other things the patroness of such domestic skills as spinning.

80–81. *made her . . . compare*] i.e., any woman brought for comparison of beauty by natural or cosmetic means would be abashed at her inferiority.

89–90. *thou . . . already*] by which you as good as have her.

91. *and learn me that*] if you will teach me that.

93. *brave*] excellent.

94. *nigromancer*] necromancer.

95. *costermongers*] apple-vendors.

thee; and I'll to the court and I'll prince it out, and he shall make thee either a silken purse, full of gold, or else a fine wrought smock.

EDWARD.

But how shall I have the maid?

RAFE.

Marry, sirrah, if thou beest a silken purse full of gold, then on Sundays she'll hang thee by her side, and you must not say a word. Now, sir, when she comes into a great press of people, for fear of the cutpurse, on a sudden she'll swap thee into her plackerd; then, sirrah, being there, you may plead for yourself.

ERMSBY.

Excellent policy!

EDWARD.

But how if I be a wrought smock?

RAFE.

Then she'll put thee into her chest and lay thee into lavender, and upon some good day she'll put thee on, and at night when you go to bed, then being turn'd from a smock to a man, you may make up the match.

LACY.

Wonderfully wisely counseled, Rafe.

EDWARD.

Rafe shall have a new coat.

RAFE.

God thank you when I have it on my back, Ned.

EDWARD.

Lacy, the fool hath laid a perfect plot;
For why our country Margaret is so coy
And stands so much upon her honest points,
That marriage or no market with the maid,
Ermsby, it must be nigromantic spells
And charms of art that must enchain her love,

---

107. *swap*] "to move something quickly or briskly" (*OED*).
107. *plackerd*] placket; a slit in a skirt or petticoat.
119. *For why*] because. 119. *coy*] modest.
120. *honest points*] chaste principles.
123. *art*] commonly, the art of sorcery.

Or else shall Edward never win the girl.
Therefore, my wags, we'll horse us in the morn,
And post to Oxford to this jolly friar.
Bacon shall by his magic do this deed.

WARREN.

Content, my lord; and that's a speedy way
To wean these headstrong puppies from the teat.

EDWARD.

I am unknown, not taken for the prince;
They only deem us frolic courtiers
That revel thus among our liege's game;
Therefore I have devised a policy.
Lacy, thou know'st next Friday is Saint James',
And then the country flocks to Harleston fair;
Then will the keeper's daughter frolic there,
And over-shine the troop of all the maids
That come to see and to be seen that day.
Haunt thee disguis'd among the country swains;
Feign th'art a farmer's son not far from thence;
Espy her loves, and who she liketh best;
Cote him, and court her to control the clown.
Say that the courtier 'tired all in green,
That help'd her handsomely to run her cheese
And fill'd her father's lodge with venison,
Commends him, and sends fairings to herself.
Buy something worthy of her parentage,
Not worth her beauty, for, Lacy, then the fair
Affords no jewel fitting for the maid.
And when thou talkest of me, note if she blush;
Oh, then she loves; but if her cheeks wax pale,
Disdain it is. Lacy, send how she fares,
And spare no time nor cost to win her loves.

---

131. *only deem us*] deem us only (example of common transposition of adverbs).
134. *Saint James'*] St. James's day is July 25.
135. *Harleston*] a small parish some four miles north of Fressingfield.
141. *loves*] fancies. 142. *Cote*] out-do. 142. *control*] deny.
142. *clown*] country bumpkin.
146. *him*] himself. 146. *fairings*] gifts bought at the fair.
152. *send*] send news of.

LACY.
I will, my lord, so execute this charge
As if that Lacy were in love with her.

EDWARD.
Send letters speedily to Oxford of the news.

RAFE.
And sirrah Lacy, buy me a thousand thousand million of fine bells.

LACY.
What wilt thou do with them, Rafe?

RAFE.
Marry, every time that Ned sighs for the keeper's daughter, I'll tie a bell about him; and so within three or four days I will send word to his father Harry that his son and my master Ned is become love's morris-dance.

EDWARD.
Well, Lacy, look with care unto thy charge,
And I will haste to Oxford to the friar,
That he by art, and thou by secret gifts,
Mayst make me lord of merry Fressingfield.

LACY.
God send your honor your heart's desire. *Exeunt.*

[ii]

Enter Friar Bacon *with* Miles, *his poor scholar, with books under his arm; with them* Burden, Mason, Clement, *three doctors.*

BACON.
Miles, where are you?

MILES.
Hic sum, dostissime et reverendissime doctor.

161. and so within] *Q1*; so within *Q2*; so that in *Q3*.

---

163. *morris-dance*] a rural dance distantly imitative of a "Moorish" dance, usually with bells sewn on the dancers' costumes.

[Scene ii]

0.1. *his poor scholar*] a poor student who would receive free board and tuition in return for menial services; a subsizar.

2. "Here I am, most learned and venerable doctor."

BACON.

Attulisti nos libros meos de necromantia?

MILES.

Ecce quam bonum et quam jocundum, habitares libros in unum.

BACON.

Now, masters of our academic state,
That rule in Oxford, viceroys in your place,
Whose heads contain maps of the liberal arts,
Spending your time in depth of learned skill,
Why flock you thus to Bacon's secret cell,
A friar newly stall'd in Brazen-nose?
Say what's your mind, that I may make reply.

BURDEN.

Bacon, we hear that long we have suspect,
That thou art read in magic's mystery;
In pyromancy to divine by flames;
To tell by hydromantic ebbs and tides;
By aeromancy to discover doubts,
To plain out questions, as Apollo did.

BACON.

Well, Master Burden, what of all this?

16. hydromantic] *Dickinson*; Hadromaticke *Q1–3*.

---

3. "Have you brought us my books of black magic?" (Here and elsewhere the Latin of the 1594 quarto is reproduced, although it is not always accurate.)

4–5. "Behold, how good and pleasant it is to dwell together among books!" (a parody of Psalms cxxxiii:1, with *libros* substituted for *fratres*).

11. *stall'd*] established.

11. *Brazen-nose*] Brasenose College, Oxford; over the College gate was (and is) a grotesque brass face with a large nose.

13. *that*] that which.

15. *pyromancy*] the art of prophesying from fire.

16. *tell*] foretell.

16. *hydromantic*] here used as a noun; hydromancy, the art of prophesying by water.

17. *discover doubts*] explain difficult propositions.

18. *plain out*] explain.

18. *as Apollo did*] This god had an oracular shrine at Delphi.

MILES.

Marry, sir, he doth but fulfill by rehearsing of these names the Fable of the Fox and the Grapes: that which is above us pertains nothing to us.

BURDEN.

I tell thee, Bacon, Oxford makes report,
Nay, England, and the court of Henry says
Th'art making of a brazen head by art
Which shall unfold strange doubts and aphorisms
And read a lecture in philosophy,
And by the help of devils and ghastly fiends,
Thou mean'st, ere many years or days be past,
To compass England with a wall of brass.

BACON.

And what of this?

MILES.

What of this, master? Why, he doth speak mystically, for he knows if your skill fail to make a brazen head, yet Mother Waters' strong ale will fit his turn to make him have a copper nose.

CLEMENT.

Bacon, we come not grieving at thy skill,
But joying that our academy yields
A man suppos'd the wonder of the world;
For if thy cunning work these miracles,
England and Europe shall admire thy fame,
And Oxford shall in characters of brass
And statues such as were built up in Rome
Eternize Friar Bacon for his art.

MASON.

Then, gentle friar, tell us thy intent.

BACON.

Seeing you come as friends unto the friar,

---

26. *aphorisms*] rules.
32. *mystically*] allegorically, in figures (cf. xvi.63).
34. *Mother Waters' strong ale*] probably an allusion to some popular alewife.
35. *copper nose*] i.e., the red nose of a drunkard.
40. *admire*] wonder at.

Resolve you, doctors, Bacon can by books
Make storming Boreas thunder from his cave
And dim fair Luna to a dark eclipse.
The great arch-ruler, potentate of hell,
Trembles, when Bacon bids him or his fiends
Bow to the force of his pentageron.
What art can work, the frolic friar knows;
And therefore will I turn my magic books
And strain out nigromancy to the deep.
I have contriv'd and fram'd a head of brass
(I made Belcephon hammer out the stuff),
And that by art shall read philosophy;
And I will strengthen England by my skill,
That if ten Caesars liv'd and reign'd in Rome,
With all the legions Europe doth contain,
They should not touch a grass of English ground.
The work that Ninus rear'd at Babylon,
The brazen walls fram'd by Semiramis,
Carved out like to the portal of the sun,
Shall not be such as rings the English strond
From Dover to the market place of Rye.

BURDEN.

Is this possible?

MILES.

I'll bring ye two or three witnesses.

BURDEN.

What be those?

---

46. *Resolve you*] assure yourselves.

47. *Boreas . . . cave*] the north wind, imprisoned in the cave of Æolus (*Aeneid* I.50–59).

51. *pentageron*] properly, "pentagonon," a five-pointed emblem, an ancient symbol of perfection, used in magic to control demons.

56. *Belcephon*] A name not found in occult books; Greene probably invented it from "Baal-zephon" (Exodus xiv:2, Numbers xxxiii:7).

62–63. These structures are described in Herodotus (I.184, III.155) and Ovid (*Met.* IV.58).

64. *portal of the sun*] the gates of Phoebus' palace, in bronze and gold (Ovid *Met.* II.1–4).

65. *strond*] strand, coast.

MILES.

Marry, sir, three or four as honest devils and good companions as any be in hell.

MASON.

No doubt but magic may do much in this,
For he that reads but mathematic rules
Shall find conclusions that avail to work
Wonders that pass the common sense of men.

BURDEN.

But Bacon roves a bow beyond his reach,
And tells of more than magic can perform,
Thinking to get a fame by fooleries.
Have I not pass'd as far in state of schools,
And read of many secrets? Yet to think
That heads of brass can utter any voice,
Or more, to tell of deep philosophy—
This is a fable Aesop had forgot.

BACON.

Burden, thou wrong'st me in detracting thus;
Bacon loves not to stuff himself with lies.
But tell me 'fore these doctors, if thou dare,
Of certain questions I shall move to thee.

BURDEN.

I will; ask what thou can.

MILES.

Marry, sir, he'll straight be on your pick-pack to know whether the feminine or the masculine gender be most worthy.

70. as] *Q1–2*; of the *Q3*. 79. far] *Q1–2*; fare *Q3*.

---

73. *mathematic*] astrological, astronomical.

75. *common sense*] ordinary perceptions.

76. *roves a bow*] stretching or aiming a bow perhaps too large; i.e., tries to perform more than lies within his reach.

79. *in state of schools*] in academic honors.

89. *pick-pack*] pickaback; i.e., "he'll be at you at once."

90–91. *whether . . . most worthy*] an ironic allusion to William Lyly's Latin grammar in which it was maintained that the masculine gender is more worthy than the feminine, and the feminine more than the neuter.

BACON.

Were you not yesterday, Master Burden, at Henley upon the Thames?

BURDEN.

I was; what then?

BACON.

What book studied you thereon all night?

BURDEN

I? None at all; I read not there a line.

BACON.

Then, doctors, Friar Bacon's art knows naught.

CLEMENT.

What say you to this, Master Burden? Doth he not touch you?

BURDEN.

I pass not of his frivolous speeches.

MILES.

Nay, Master Burden, my master, ere he hath done with you, will turn you from a doctor to a dunce, and shake you so small that he will leave no more learning in you than is in Balaam's ass.

BACON.

Masters, for that learned Burden's skill is deep,
And sore he doubts of Bacon's cabalism,
I'll show you why he haunts to Henley oft:
Not, doctors, for to taste the fragrant air,
But there to spend the night in alchemy,
To multiply with secret spells of art.
Thus private steals he learning from us all.
To prove my sayings true, I'll show you straight

93. the] *Q1; not in Q1–2.*
106. sore] *Q1–3; various eds. emend to* for.
112. sayings] *Q1*; saying *Q2–3.*

---

92. *Henley*] about twenty miles from Oxford.
100. *pass not of*] care not for.
104. *Balaam's ass*] alluding to the story in Numbers xxii:22–34; Miles tells Burden that Bacon will strike the fear of God into him with his wizardry.
106. *cabalism*] secret art.

The book he keeps at Henley for himself.

MILES.

Nay, now my master goes to conjuration, take heed.

BACON.

Masters, stand still; fear not. I'll show you but his book.

Here he conjures.

Per omnes deos infernales, Belcephon.

Enter a woman *with a shoulder of mutton on a spit, and a devil.*

MILES.

Oh, master, cease your conjuration, or you spoil all, for here's a she-devil come with a shoulder of mutton on a spit. You have marr'd the devil's supper; but no doubt he thinks our college fare is slender, and so hath sent you his cook with a shoulder of mutton to make it exceed.

HOSTESS.

Oh, where am I, or what's become of me?

BACON.

What art thou?

HOSTESS.

Hostess at Henley, mistress of the Bell.

BACON.

How camest thou here?

HOSTESS.

As I was in the kitchen 'mongst the maids,
Spitting the meat against supper for my guess,
A motion moved me to look forth of door.
No sooner had I pried into the yard,
But straight a whirlwind hoisted me from thence
And mounted me aloft unto the clouds.
As in a trance, I thought nor feared naught,

115. *Masters, stand still*] an implicit S.D., indicating a frightened movement among the doctors.

115.1. *conjures*] stage business here would involve describing with a staff or wand the magic circle, probably followed by gestures.

116. "By all the infernal gods, Belcephon."

121. *exceed*] improve.

127. *against*] in expectation of, in provision for (cf. ix.159–160).

127. *guess*] guests (obsolete form).

128. *motion*] impulse.

129. *pried*] peered out.

Nor know I where or whither I was ta'en,
Nor where I am, nor what these persons be.

BACON.

No? Know you not Master Burden?

HOSTESS.

Oh, yes, good sir, he is my daily guest.
What, Master Burden, 'twas but yesternight
That you and I at Henley play'd at cards.

BURDEN.

I know not what we did; a pox of all conjuring friars!

CLEMENT.

Now, jolly friar, tell us, is this the book
That Burden is so careful to look on?

BACON.

It is; but, Burden, tell me now,
Thinkest thou that Bacon's nigromantic skill
Cannot perform his head and wall of brass,
When he can fetch thine hostess in such post?

MILES.

I'll warrant you, master, if Master Burden could conjure as well as you, he would have his book every night from Henley to study on at Oxford.

MASON.

Burden, what, are you mated by this frolic friar?
Look how he droops; his guilty conscience
Drives him to bash and makes his hostess blush.

BACON.

Well, mistress, for I will not have you miss'd,
You shall to Henley to cheer up your guests
'Fore supper 'gin. Burden, bid her adieu,
Say farewell to your hostess 'fore she goes.
Sirrah, away, and set her safe at home.

HOSTESS.

Master Burden, when shall we see you at Henley?

Exeunt Hostess *and the devil.*

145. thine] *Q1–2*; thy *Q3*. 156. safe] *Q1–2*; selfe *Q3*.

---

145. *post*] speed. 149. *mated*] put down. 151. *bash*] shame.

BURDEN.

The devil take thee and Henley too.

MILES.

Master, shall I make a good motion?

BACON.

What's that?

MILES.

Marry, sir, now that my hostess is gone to provide supper, conjure up another spirit, and send Doctor Burden flying after.

BACON.

Thus, rulers of our academic state,
You have seen the friar frame his art by proof;
And as the college called Brazen-nose
Is under him, and he the master there,
So surely shall this head of brass be fram'd,
And yield forth strange and uncouth aphorisms;
And hell and Hecate shall fail the friar,
But I will circle England round with brass.

MILES.

So be it, *et nunc et semper*. Amen. *Exeunt omnes.*

[iii]

Enter Margaret, *the fair maid of Fressingfield, with* Thomas, [Richard,] *and* Joan, *and other clowns;* Lacy, *disguised in country apparel.*

THOMAS.

By my troth, Margaret, here's a weather is able to make

162. up] *Q1; not in Q2–3.*

[Scene iii]
0.2. *Richard*] *not in Q1–3.*

---

159. *motion*] proposal.

169. *uncouth*] strange, marvelous.

170. *Hecate*] originally a moon goddess, a variety of witch in medieval legends of sorcery; here trisyllabic.

172. *et . . . semper*] "both now and forevermore"; parody of the liturgy.

[Scene iii]

1. *is able*] that is able.

a man call his father whoreson. If this weather hold, we shall have hay good cheap, and butter and cheese at Harleston will bear no price.

MARGARET.

Thomas, maids, when they come to see the fair,
Count not to make a cope for dearth of hay.
When we have turn'd our butter to the salt,
And set our cheese safely upon the racks,
Then let our fathers price it as they please.
We country sluts of merry Fressingfield
Come to buy needless naughts to make us fine,
And look that young men should be frank this day,
And court us with such fairings as they can.
Phoebus is blithe, and frolic looks from heaven
As when he courted lovely Semele,
Swearing the pedlars shall have empty packs,
If that fair weather may make chapmen buy.

LACY.

But, lovely Peggy, Semele is dead,
And therefore Phoebus from his palace pries,
And, seeing such a sweet and seemly saint,
Shows all his glories for to court yourself.

MARGARET.

This is a fairing, gentle sir, indeed,
To soothe me up with such smooth flattery;
But learn of me, your scoff's too broad before.
Well, Joan, our beauties must abide their jests;
We serve the turn in jolly Fressingfield.

8. safely] *Q1; not in Q2–3.*
9. price] prise *Q1–3.*
21. glories] *Q1*; glory *Q2–3.*

3. *good cheap*] at a low price.
6. *cope*] bargain.
10. *sluts*] simple girls (no pejorative connotation).
11. *naughts*] trifles.
12. *look that*] expect that.
12. *frank*] generous.
15. Zeus, not Phoebus, courted Semele.
17. *chapmen*] pedlars.
23. *soothe me up*] humor me.
24. *too broad before*] much too unsubtle.

JOAN.

Margaret, a farmer's daughter for a farmer's son.
I warrant you the meanest of us both
Shall have a mate to lead us from the church.
But, Thomas, what's the news? What, in a dump?
Give me your hand, we are near a pedlar's shop;
Out with your purse; we must have fairings now.

THOMAS.

Faith, Joan, and shall. I'll bestow a fairing on you, and then we will to the tavern and snap off a pint of wine or two.

All this while Lacy *whispers* Margaret *in the ear.*

MARGARET.

Whence are you, sir? Of Suffolk? For your terms
Are finer than the common sort of men.

LACY.

Faith, lovely girl, I am of Beccles by,
Your neighbor not above six miles from hence,
A farmer's son that never was so quaint
But that he could do courtesy to such dames.
But trust me, Margaret, I am sent in charge
From him that revel'd in your father's house,
And fill'd his lodge with cheer and venison,
'Tired in green. He sent you this rich purse,
His token that he help'd you run your cheese,
And in the milkhouse chatted with yourself.

MARGARET.

To me? You forget yourself.

LACY.

Women are often weak in memory.

34. will to] *Q1–2*; will go to *Q3*.

---

33. *shall*] i.e., you shall.
36. *terms*] phrases, rhetoric.
36–54. Margaret and Lacy would stand in a different portion of the stage for this exchange; Joan and Thomas do not leave the stage.
38. *Beccles*] a small Suffolk market-town just northeast of Harleston.
38. *by*] hard-by.
40. *quaint*] shy, countrified.
48. *You forget yourself*] i.e., you are mistaken.

MARGARET.

Oh, pardon, sir, I call to mind the man.
'Twere little manners to refuse his gift,
And yet I hope he sends it not for love;
For we have little leisure to debate of that.

JOAN.

What, Margaret, blush not; maids must have their loves.

THOMAS.

Nay, by the mass, she looks pale as if she were angry.

RICHARD.

Sirrah, are you of Beccles? I pray, how doth Goodman Cob? My father bought a horse of him. I'll tell you, Marget, 'a were good to be a gentleman's jade, for of all things the foul hilding could not abide a dungcart.

MARGARET [*aside*].

How different is this farmer from the rest
That erst as yet hath pleas'd my wand'ring sight.
His words are witty, quickened with a smile,
His courtesy gentle, smelling of the court;
Facile and debonair in all his deeds,
Proportion'd as was Paris, when, in gray,
He courted Œnon in the vale by Troy.
Great lords have come and pleaded for my love—
Who but the keeper's lass of Fressingfield?
And yet methinks this farmer's jolly son
Passeth the proudest that hath pleas'd mine eye.
But, Peg, disclose not that thou art in love,
And show as yet no sign of love to him,
Although thou well wouldst wish him for thy love;

---

56. *Goodman*] popular term for the head of a family.

58. *'a*] he.

58,59. *jade . . . hilding*] contemptuous names for a worthless horse, a nag.

61. *erst as yet*] hitherto. 62. *quickened*] enlivened.

65. *Paris . . . in gray*] Gray was the traditional color for the garb of literary shepherds.

66. *Œnon*] a nymph of Mt. Ida loved and deserted by Paris before his adventure with Helen.

69. *jolly*] fresh, gay (from Fr. *joli*).

70. *proudest*] most splendid.

Keep that to thee, till time doth serve thy turn
To show the grief wherein thy heart doth burn.
Come, Joan and Thomas, shall we to the fair?
You, Beccles man, will not forsake us now?

LACY.
Not whilst I may have such quaint girls as you.

MARGARET.
Well, if you chance to come by Fressingfield,
Make but a step into the keeper's lodge,
And such poor fare as woodmen can afford—
Butter and cheese, cream, and fat venison—
You shall have store, and welcome therewithal.

LACY.
Gramercies, Peggy; look for me ere long. *Exeunt omnes.*

[iv]

Enter [King] Henry the Third; *the* Emperor [of Germany]; *the* King of Castile; Eleanor, *his daughter;* Jacques Vandermast, *a German* [*scientist*].

HENRY.
Great men of Europe, monarchs of the west,
Ring'd with the walls of old Oceanus,
Whose lofty surge is like the battlements
That compass'd high-built Babel in with towers,
Welcome, my lords, welcome, brave western kings,
To England's shore, whose promontory cleeves
Shows Albion is another little world.
Welcome says English Henry to you all;
Chiefly unto the lovely Eleanor,
Who dar'd for Edward's sake cut through the seas,

[Scene iv]
3. surge is] *Dyce*; surges *Q1–3*.

---

75. *grief*] love's pain, a traditional conceit.
83. *store*] enough, plenty.

[Scene iv]
0.1. *Emperor of Germany*] Frederick II, brother-in-law to Henry III.
2. *Oceanus*] In Greek cosmology, the river supposed to encircle the plain of the earth, also personified as one of the Titans.

And venture as Agenor's damsel through the deep,
To get the love of Henry's wanton son.

CASTILE.

England's rich monarch, brave Plantagenet,
The Pyren Mounts swelling above the clouds,
That ward the wealthy Castile in with walls,
Could not detain the beauteous Eleanor;
But hearing of the fame of Edward's youth,
She dar'd to brook Neptunus' haughty pride
And bide the brunt of froward Æolus.
Then may fair England welcome her the more.

ELEANOR.

After that English Henry, by his lords,
Had sent Prince Edward's lovely counterfeit,
A present to the Castile Eleanor,
The comely portrait of so brave a man,
The virtuous fame discoursed of his deeds,
Edward's courageous resolution
Done at the Holy Land 'fore Damas' walls,
Led both mine eye and thoughts in equal links
To like so of the English monarch's son
That I attempted perils for his sake.

EMPEROR.

Where is the prince, my lord?

HENRY.

He posted down, not long since, from the court

23. Castile] *Q1–2*; costly *Q3*.

25. discoursed] *Q1–2*; discovered *Q3*.

---

11. *Agenor's damsel*] Europa, carried off across the sea by Zeus, who had taken the form of a bull.

12. *wanton*] amorous.

14. *Pyren Mounts*] the Pyrenees.

18. *haughty pride*] perhaps, as well as the literal meaning, with a suggestion of the height of the waves; swelling waters could be called "proud."

19. *froward*] untoward, adverse.

19. *Æolus*] god of winds.

22. *lovely*] lovable, amorous.

22. *counterfeit*] portrait.

27. *Damas'*] Damascus.

To Suffolk side, to merry Framingham,
To sport himself amongst my fallow deer;
From thence, by packets sent to Hampton House,
We hear the prince is ridden with his lords
To Oxford, in the academy there
To hear dispute amongst the learned men.
But we will send forth letters for my son,
To will him come from Oxford to the court.

EMPEROR.

Nay, rather, Henry, let us, as we be,
Ride for to visit Oxford with our train.
Fain would I see your universities
And what learned men your academy yields.
From Hapsburg have I brought a learned clerk
To hold dispute with English orators.
This doctor, surnam'd Jacques Vandermast,
A German born, pass'd into Padua,
To Florence, and to fair Bolonia,
To Paris, Rheims, and stately Orleans,
And, talking there with men of art, put down
The chiefest of them all in aphorisms,
In magic, and the mathematic rules.
Now let us, Henry, try him in your schools.

HENRY.

He shall, my lord; this motion likes me well.

45. Hapsburg] ***Collier, Dyce***; Haspurg *Q1–3, Gayley*; Augsburg *suggested by W. L. Renwick.*

---

33. *side*] border.

33. *Framingham*] Framlingham, in southern Suffolk; the spelling of the quartos indicates pronunciation (Fremingham).

34. *fallow*] reddish yellow.

35. *Hampton House*] built by Wolsey, later a royal residence.

38. *dispute*] learned debate.

45. *Hapsburg*] the famous house which began a long period of power and influence shortly after the reign of Frederick, who was a renowned patron of learning.

47. *Jacques*] perhaps with a pun on "jakes," a privy.

48. *pass'd into*] journeyed through.

48–50. *Padua . . . Orleans*] cities with universities or academies.

We'll progress straight to Oxford with our trains,
And see what men our academy brings.
And, wonder Vandermast, welcome to me;
In Oxford shalt thou find a jolly friar
Called Friar Bacon, England's only flower.
Set him but nonplus in his magic spells,
And make him yield in mathematic rules,
And for thy glory I will bind thy brows
Not with a poet's garland made of bays,
But with a coronet of choicest gold.
Whilst then we fit to Oxford with our troops,
Let's in and banquet in our English court. [*Exeunt.*]

[v]

Enter Rafe Simnell *in Edward's apparel;* Edward, Warren, Ermsby, *disguised.*

RAFE.

Where be these vagabond knaves, that they attend no better on their master?

EDWARD.

If it please your honor, we are all ready at an inch.

RAFE.

Sirrah, Ned, I'll have no more post horse to ride on. I'll have another fetch.

ERMSBY.

I pray you, how is that, my lord?

RAFE.

Marry, sir, I'll send to the Isle of Ely for four or five

66. fit] *Q1*; sit *Q2–3*.

---

56. *progress*] journey in state.
66. *fit*] make ready (cf. ix.169).

[Scene v]
3. *at an inch*] at any instant, at your beck and call.
5. *fetch*] trick.
7. *Isle of Ely*] in Elizabethan times an undrained swamp in the county of Cambridge.

dozen of geese, and I'll have them tied six and six together with whipcord. Now upon their backs will I have a fair field-bed with a canopy; and so, when it is my pleasure, I'll flee into what place I please. This will be easy.

WARREN.

Your honor hath said well; but shall we to Brazen-nose College before we pull off our boots?

ERMSBY.

Warren, well motioned; we will to the friar
Before we revel it within the town.
Rafe, see you keep your countenance like a prince.

RAFE.

Wherefore have I such a company of cutting knaves to wait upon me, but to keep and defend my countenance against all mine enemies? Have you not good swords and bucklers?

Enter Bacon *and* Miles.

ERMSBY.

Stay, who comes here?

WARREN.

Some scholar; and we'll ask him where Friar Bacon is.

BACON.

Why, thou arrant dunce, shall I never make thee good scholar? Doth not all the town cry out and say, Friar Bacon's subsizar is the greatest blockhead in all Oxford? Why, thou canst not speak one word of true Latin.

MILES.

No, sir? Yes; what is this else? *Ego sum tuus homo,* "I

28. Yes] *Q1–2; not in Q3.*

---

11. *flee*] fly.
17. *keep your countenance*] hold your expression; usage suggestive of a formalized facial expression appropriate to a theatrical role.
18. *cutting*] swaggering.
19. *countenance*] here, person.

am your man." I warrant you, sir, as good Tully's phrase as any is in Oxford.

BACON.

Come on, sirrah, what part of speech is *Ego*?

MILES.

Ego, that is "I"; marry, *nomen substantivo.*

BACON.

How prove you that?

MILES.

Why, sir, let him prove himself and 'a will; "I" can be heard, felt, and understood.

BACON.

Oh, gross dunce!

Here beat him.

EDWARD.

Come, let us break off this dispute between these two. Sirrah, where is Brazen-nose College?

MILES.

Not far from Coppersmiths' Hall.

EDWARD.

What, dost thou mock me?

MILES.

Not I, sir; but what would you at Brazen-nose?

ERMSBY.

Marry, we would speak with Friar Bacon.

31. on] *Q1; not in Q2–3.*

35. heard] *Q1–3 print* hard, *meaning* heard.

---

29. *Tully's phrase*] Cicero's; i.e., as good Ciceronian Latin, complex and rhetorical.

29–32. *Tully's . . . nomen substantivo*] see the description of the Pedant, in the *Overburian Characters* (1614): "He dares not thinke a thought, that the Nominative case governes not the verbe; and he never had meaning in his life, for he travelled onely for words. His ambition is *Criticisme,* and his example is *Tully.* Hee values phrases, and elects them by the sound, and the eight parts of speech are his servants."

39. *Coppersmiths' Hall*] a joking reference to some tavern (?).

MILES.

Whose men be you?

ERMSBY.

Marry, scholar, here's our master.

RAFE.

Sirrah, I am the master of these good fellows; mayst thou not know me to be a lord by my reparel?

MILES.

Then here's good game for the hawk; for here's the master fool and a covey of coxcombs. One wise man, I think, would spring you all.

EDWARD.

Gog's wounds! Warren, kill him.

WARREN.

Why, Ned, I think the devil be in my sheath; I cannot get out my dagger.

ERMSBY.

Nor I mine. 'Swones, Ned, I think I am bewitch'd.

MILES.

A company of scabs. The proudest of you all draw your weapon, if he can. [*Aside.*] See how boldly I speak, now my master is by.

EDWARD.

I strive in vain; but if my sword be shut
And conjured fast by magic in my sheath,
Villain, here is my fist.

Strike him a box on the ear.

MILES.

Oh, I beseech you, conjure his hands, too, that he may not lift his arms to his head, for he is light-fingered.

60. hands] *Q1*; hand *Q2–3*.

---

46. *reparel*] apparel.

47–48. *master fool . . . coxcombs*] The scoff would be directed at the prince, disguised as the fool and wearing his coxcomb cap.

49. *spring*] to cause birds to fly from cover.

50. *Gog's*] God's. 53. *'Swones*] God's wounds. 54. *scabs*] scoundrels.

61. *light-fingered*] the cant term for the skill of a pickpocket or cutpurse.

RAFE.

Ned, strike him. I'll warrant thee by mine honor.

BACON.

What means the English prince to wrong my man?

EDWARD.

To whom speakest thou?

BACON.

To thee.

EDWARD.

Who art thou?

BACON.

Could you not judge when all your swords grew fast
That Friar Bacon was not far from hence?
Edward, King Henry's son, and Prince of Wales,
Thy fool disguis'd cannot conceal thyself.
I know both Ermsby and the Sussex earl,
Else Friar Bacon had but little skill.
Thou comest in post from merry Fressingfield,
Fast-fancied to the keeper's bonny lass,
To crave some succor of the jolly friar;
And Lacy, Earl of Lincoln, hast thou left
To 'treat fair Margaret to allow thy loves;
But friends are men, and love can baffle lords.
The earl both woos and courts her for himself.

WARREN.

Ned, this is strange; the friar knoweth all.

ERMSBY.

Apollo could not utter more than this.

EDWARD.

I stand amazed to hear this jolly friar
Tell even the very secrets of my thoughts.
But, learned Bacon, since thou knowest the cause
Why I did post so fast from Fressingfield,

79. woos] *Q2–3*; woes *Q1*.
80. knoweth] *Q1–2*; knows *Q3*.
82. hear this] *Q1–2*; hear of this *Q3*.

---

71. *Sussex earl*] Warren.
74. *Fast-fancied*] bound with passions.
77. *'treat*] entreat.

Help, friar, at a pinch, that I may have
The love of lovely Margaret to myself,
And, as I am true Prince of Wales, I'll give
Living and lands to strength thy college state.

WARREN.

Good friar, help the prince in this.

RAFE.

Why, servant Ned, will not the friar do it? Were not my sword glued to my scabbard by conjuration, I would cut off his head, and make him do it by force.

MILES.

In faith, my lord, your manhood and your sword is all alike; they are so fast conjured that we shall never see them.

ERMSBY.

What, doctor, in a dump? Tush, help the prince,
And thou shalt see how liberal he will prove.

BACON.

Crave not such actions greater dumps than these?
I will, my lord, strain out my magic spells;
For this day comes the earl to Fressingfield,
And 'fore that night shuts in the day with dark,
They'll be betrothed each to other fast.
But come with me; we'll to my study straight,
And in a glass prospective I will show
What's done this day in merry Fressingfield.

EDWARD.

Gramercies, Bacon; I will quite thy pain.

88. true] *Q1–2*; the *Q3*.
94–95. is all alike] *all copies of Q1 except Huntington Library, which omits* is.
102. shuts] *Q1–2*; shut *Q3*.

---

86. *at a pinch*] in an emergency.
89. *strength*] strengthen.
89. *college state*] the holdings and properties of Brasenose.
105. *glass prospective*] properly, perspective; Bacon's mirror-like magic property; perhaps the form of the word used suggests that which looks forward, whether into the future or the distance.
107. *quite*] requite.

BACON.

But send your train, my lord, into the town;
My scholar shall go bring them to their inn.
Meanwhile we'll see the knavery of the earl.

EDWARD.

Warren, leave me; and, Ermsby, take the fool;
Let him be master, and go revel it
Till I and Friar Bacon talk awhile.

WARREN.

We will, my lord.

RAFE.

Faith, Ned, and I'll lord it out till thou comest. I'll be Prince of Wales over all the blackpots in Oxford.

Exeunt [*all except* Bacon *and* Edward].

[vi] Bacon *and* Edward *goes into the study.*

BACON.

Now, frolic Edward, welcome to my cell.
Here tempers Friar Bacon many toys,
And holds this place his consistory court,

108. your] *Q1–2*; thy *Q3*.
108. into] *Q1–2*; unto *Q3*.
109. go bring] *Q1–2*; go and bring *Q3*.

---

116. *blackpots*] jugs for wine covered with or made from black leather.

[Scene vi]

0.1. *goes into the study*] It is doubtful that any specific portion of the stage would have represented the "study" throughout the play; at this point, after the exit of Rafe, Miles, and the prince's train, Bacon and Edward simply may have walked a few paces into a new acting area, never leaving the stage. In the anonymous *George a Greene* (probably by Greene), there is an identical method of scene transition, revealing Elizabethan stage practice: "*Shoemaker*. Come, sir, will you go to the town's end now, sir?/ *Jenkin*. Ay, sir, come./ Now we are at town's end, what say you now?" Clearly, the two actors have simply walked across the stage.

2. *tempers*] compounds, mixes.

3. *consistory court*] the court of the diocesan bishop, held by the bishop's chancellor.

Wherein the devils pleads homage to his words.
Within this glass prospective thou shalt see
This day what's done in merry Fressingfield
'Twixt lovely Peggy and the Lincoln earl.

EDWARD.

Friar, thou glad'st me. Now shall Edward try
How Lacy meaneth to his sovereign lord.

BACON.

Stand there and look directly in the glass.

Enter Margaret *and* Friar Bungay.

What sees my lord?

EDWARD.

I see the keeper's lovely lass appear
As bright-sun as the paramour of Mars,
Only attended by a jolly friar.

BACON.

Sit still, and keep the crystal in your eye.

MARGARET.

But tell me, Friar Bungay, is it true
That this fair courteous country swain,
Who says his father is a farmer nigh,
Can be Lord Lacy, Earl of Lincolnshire?

BUNGAY.

Peggy, 'tis true, 'tis Lacy, for my life,
Or else mine art and cunning both doth fail,
Left by Prince Edward to procure his loves;
For he in green that holp you run your cheese

4. pleads] *Q1*; plead *Q2–3*.
13. bright-sun] *Q1–3, Gayley, Baskervill*; brightsome *conj. Collier, Dyce*; sun-bright *conj. Gayley*.
21. doth] *Q1,3*; do *Q2*.
23. holp] *Q1–2*; help *Q3*.

---

9. *meaneth*] is disposed toward.
13. *bright-sun*] brightsome (?); see textual note.
13. *paramour of Mars*] Venus.
14. *Only attended*] attended only.
15. *eye*] sight.
23. *holp*] helped.

Is son to Henry, and the Prince of Wales.

MARGARET.

Be what he will, his lure is but for lust.
But did Lord Lacy like poor Margaret,
Or would he deign to wed a country lass,
Friar, I would his humble handmaid be,
And, for great wealth, quite him with courtesy.

BUNGAY.

Why, Margaret, dost thou love him?

MARGARET.

His personage, like the pride of vaunting Troy,
Might well avouch to shadow Helen's scape;
His wit is quick, and ready in conceit,
As Greece afforded in her chiefest prime;
Courteous, ah, friar, full of pleasing smiles.
Trust me, I love too much to tell thee more;
Suffice to me he is England's paramour.

BUNGAY.

Hath not each eye that view'd thy pleasing face
Surnamed thee Fair Maid of Fressingfield?

MARGARET.

Yes, Bungay, and would God the lovely earl
Had that in *esse* that so many sought.

25. lure] *Q1–2*; love *Q3*.
30. thou] *Q1*; *not in Q2–3*.
32. scape] *Gayley, Neilson*; cape *Q1–3, Collier*; rape *conj. Collier, Dyce, Ward*.
37. England's] *Q1–2*; English *Q3*.

---

25. *lure*] temptation; in the art of falconry, a bunch of feathers on a cord, within which the hawk finds food (Edward first saw Margaret while hunting).

31. *pride . . . Troy*] Paris.

32. *shadow*] to protect, excuse.

32. *scape*] possibly "escape," but more likely in the sense of transgression, wrongdoing.

33. *conceit*] metaphorical language.

37. *England's paramour*] i.e., the best lover in England.

41. *in esse*] in actuality.

BUNGAY.

Fear not, the friar will not be behind
To show his cunning to entangle love.

EDWARD.

I think the friar courts the bonny wench.
Bacon, methinks he is a lusty churl.

BACON.

Now look, my lord.

Enter Lacy.

EDWARD.

Gog's wounds, Bacon, here comes Lacy!

BACON.

Sit still, my lord, and mark the comedy.

BUNGAY.

Here's Lacy. Margaret, step aside awhile.

LACY.

Daphne, the damsel that caught Phoebus fast,
And lock'd him in the brightness of her looks,
Was not so beauteous in Apollo's eyes
As is fair Margaret to the Lincoln earl.
Recant thee, Lacy, thou art put in trust.
Edward, thy sovereign's son, hath chosen thee,
A secret friend, to court her for himself,
And darest thou wrong thy prince with treachery?
Lacy, love makes no exception of a friend,
Nor deems it of a prince but as a man.
Honor bids thee control him in his lust;
His wooing is not for to wed the girl,
But to entrap her and beguile the lass.
Lacy, thou lovest; then brook not such abuse,
But wed her, and abide thy prince's frown,

50–52. *Daphne . . . Apollo's eyes*] Ovid (*Met.* I.452–567) tells how Phoebus Apollo chased Daphne until she was changed into a laurel tree.

56. *secret*] close, confidential.

60. *control*] curb.

For better die, than see her live disgrac'd.

MARGARET.

Come, friar, I will shake him from his dumps.
How cheer you, sir? A penny for your thought.
You're early up; pray God it be the near.
What, come from Beccles in a morn so soon?

LACY.

Thus watchful are such men as live in love,
Whose eyes brook broken slumbers for their sleep.
I tell thee, Peggy, since last Harleston fair
My mind hath felt a heap of passions.

MARGARET.

A trusty man, that court it for your friend.
Woo you still for the courtier all in green?
I marvel that he sues not for himself.

LACY.

Peggy, I pleaded first to get your grace for him,
But when mine eyes survey'd your beauteous looks,
Love, like a wag, straight dived into my heart,
And there did shrine the idea of yourself.
Pity me, though I be a farmer's son,
And measure not my riches but my love.

MARGARET.

You are very hasty; for to garden well,
Seeds must have time to sprout before they spring;
Love ought to creep as doth the dial's shade,
For timely ripe is rotten too too soon.

BUNGAY.

Deus hic; room for a merry friar.

65. better] *Q1; not in Q2–3.*

69. What, come] *Q1;* What'are come *Q2–3.*

---

68. *the near*] the nearer to your purpose (being up early).

70. *watchful*] fitful, sleepless.

80. *idea*] image.

85. *dial's shade*] shadow of a sundial.

86. *too too*] exceeding (not a repetition of "too," but a provincial expression).

87. *Deus hic*] from the Vulgate transl. of Genesis xxviii:16 ("Surely the Lord is in this place").

What, youth of Beccles, with the keeper's lass?
'Tis well. But, tell me, hear you any news?

MARGARET.

No, friar. What news?

BUNGAY.

Hear you not how the pursevants do post
With proclamations through each country town?

LACY.

For what, gentle friar? Tell the news.

BUNGAY.

Dwell'st thou in Beccles and hear'st not of these news?
Lacy, the Earl of Lincoln, is late fled
From Windsor court, disguised like a swain,
And lurks about the country here unknown.
Henry suspects him of some treachery,
And therefore doth proclaim in every way
That who can take the Lincoln earl shall have,
Paid in the Exchequer, twenty thousand crowns.

LACY.

The Earl of Lincoln! Friar, thou art mad.
It was some other; thou mistakest the man.
The Earl of Lincoln! Why, it cannot be.

MARGARET.

Yes, very well, my lord, for you are he.
The keeper's daughter took you prisoner.
Lord Lacy, yield; I'll be your jailer once.

EDWARD.

How familiar they be, Bacon.

BACON.

Sit still, and mark the sequel of their loves.

LACY.

Then am I double prisoner to thyself.
Peggy, I yield. But are these news in jest?

MARGARET.

In jest with you, but earnest unto me;
For why these wrongs do wring me at the heart.

102. thou art] *Q1–2*; art thou *Q3*.

91. *pursevants*] pursuivants; officers attending upon the heralds.

Ah, how these earls and noble men of birth
Flatter and feign to forge poor women's ill.

LACY.

Believe me, lass, I am the Lincoln earl
I not deny; but 'tired thus in rags
I lived disguis'd to win fair Peggy's love.

MARGARET.

What love is there where wedding ends not love?

LACY.

I meant, fair girl, to make thee Lacy's wife.

MARGARET.

I little think that earls will stoop so low.

LACY.

Say, shall I make thee countess ere I sleep?

MARGARET.

Handmaid unto the earl, so please himself;
A wife in name, but servant in obedience.

LACY.

The Lincoln countess, for it shall be so.
I'll plight the bands, and seal it with a kiss.

EDWARD.

Gog's wounds, Bacon, they kiss! I'll stab them!

BACON.

Oh, hold your hands, my lord, it is the glass!

EDWARD.

Choler to see the traitors 'gree so well
Made me think the shadows substances.

BACON.

'Twere a long poinard, my lord, to reach between
Oxford and Fressingfield. But sit still and see more.

BUNGAY.

Well, Lord of Lincoln, if your loves be knit,
And that your tongues and thoughts do both agree,

120. meant] *Q1–2*; meane *Q3*.

---

116. *I am*] i.e., that I am.
126. *plight the bands*] pledge myself to the marriage bans.
130. *shadows*] the images in Bacon's glass.
131. *poinard*] poniard.

To avoid ensuing jars, I'll hamper up the match.
I'll take my portace forth and wed you here;
Then go to bed and seal up your desires.

LACY.

Friar, content. Peggy, how like you this?

MARGARET.

What likes my lord is pleasing unto me.

BUNGAY.

Then handfast hand, and I will to my book.

BACON.

What sees my lord now?

EDWARD.

Bacon, I see the lovers hand in hand,
The friar ready with his portace there
To wed them both; then am I quite undone.
Bacon, help now, if e'er thy magic serv'd;
Help, Bacon; stop the marriage now,
If devils or nigromancy may suffice,
And I will give thee forty thousand crowns.

BACON.

Fear not, my lord, I'll stop the jolly friar
For mumbling up his orisons this day.

LACY.

Why speak'st not, Bungay? Friar, to thy book.

Bungay *is mute, crying, "Hud, hud."*

MARGARET.

How lookest thou, friar, as a man distraught?
Reft of thy senses, Bungay? Show by signs,
If thou be dumb, what passions holdeth thee.

LACY.

He's dumb indeed. Bacon hath with his devils

145.] *Q2–3 repeat line, with Q3 assigning it to Bacon.* 154. passions] *Q1*; passion *Q2–3.*

---

135. *jars*] discords. 135. *hamper up*] make fast quickly.
136. *portace*] a portable breviary or prayer book.
140. *handfast*] join. 150. *For*] from.
151.1. *Hud, hud*] indicating Bungay's efforts to speak.
154. *passions*] afflictions.

Enchanted him, or else some strange disease
Or apoplexy hath possess'd his lungs.
But Peggy, what he cannot with his book,
We'll 'twixt us both unite it up in heart.

MARGARET.
Else let me die, my lord, a miscreant.

EDWARD.
Why stands Friar Bungay so amaz'd?

BACON.
I have struck him dumb, my lord; and if your honor please,
I'll fetch this Bungay straightway from Fressingfield,
And he shall dine with us in Oxford here.

EDWARD.
Bacon, do that and thou contentest me.

LACY.
Of courtesy, Margaret, let us lead the friar
Unto thy father's lodge, to comfort him
With broths, to bring him from this hapless trance.

MARGARET.
Or else, my lord, we were passing unkind
To leave the friar so in his distress.

Enter a devil, and carry [*off*] Bungay *on his back.*

MARGARET.
Oh, help, my lord, a devil! a devil, my lord!
Look how he carries Bungay on his back!
Let's hence, for Bacon's spirits be abroad. *Exeunt.*

EDWARD.
Bacon, I laugh to see the jolly friar
Mounted upon the devil, and how the earl
Flees with his bonny lass for fear.
As soon as Bungay is at Brazen-nose,
And I have chatted with the merry friar,
I will in post hie me to Fressingfield
And quite these wrongs on Lacy ere it be long.

161. Bungay] *Collier*; Bacon *Q1–3*. 177.] Q1; *not in Q2–3*.
174. laugh] *Q1–2*; love *Q3*.

---

161. *amaz'd*] struck dumb.
169. *passing*] more than.

BACON.

So be it, my lord. But let us to our dinner;
For ere we have taken our repast awhile,
We shall have Bungay brought to Brazen-nose. *Exeunt.*

[vii] *Enter three doctors,* Burden, Mason, Clement.

MASON.

Now that we are gathered in the Regent House,
It fits us talk about the king's repair;
For he, troop'd with all the western kings
That lie alongst the Dansig seas by east,
North by the clime of frosty Germany,
The Almain monarch, and the Saxon duke,
Castile, and lovely Eleanor with him,
Have in their jests resolved for Oxford town.

BURDEN.

We must lay plots of stately tragedies,
Strange comic shows, such as proud Roscius
Vaunted before the Roman emperors,
To welcome all the western potentates.

[Scene vii]
6. Saxon] *conj. Collier;* Scocon *Q1–3.*
9. of] *Q1;* for *Q2–3.*
12.] *Dyce; Q1–3 assign to Clement.*

[Scene vii]

1. *Regent House*] the place of meeting for those Masters of Arts presiding over a school in one of the University faculties.

2. *repair*] approach.

3. *troop'd with*] attended by.

4. *Dansig*] Baltic.

6. *Almain*] German.

8. *jests*] revels.

9. *plots*] in the technical theatrical sense of a rough scheme or outline for performance, showing entrances, exits, properties, and the like.

9. *stately*] dignified; referring to the sort of Latin tragedies written by the scholars and sometimes performed in the college halls for the instruction of students and the entertainment of visiting dignitaries.

10. *Strange*] exotic.

10. *shows*] masques, pageants.

10. *Roscius*] a famous Roman actor of both tragedy and comedy.

CLEMENT.
But more, the king by letters hath foretold
That Frederick, the Almain emperor,
Hath brought with him a German of esteem,
Whose surname is Don Jacques Vandermast,
Skillful in magic and those secret arts.

MASON.
Then must we all make suit unto the friar,
To Friar Bacon, that he vouch this task,
And undertake to countervail in skill
The German; else there's none in Oxford can
Match and dispute with learned Vandermast.

BURDEN.
Bacon, if he will hold the German play,
We'll teach him what an English friar can do.
The devil, I think, dare not dispute with him.

CLEMENT.
Indeed, Mas Doctor, he pleasured you
In that he brought your hostess with her spit
From Henley, posting unto Brazen-nose.

BURDEN.
A vengeance on the friar for his pains;
But, leaving that, let's hie to Bacon straight
To see if he will take this task in hand.

CLEMENT.
Stay, what rumor is this? The town is up in a mutiny. What hurly-burly is this?

Enter a Constable, *with* Rafe, Warren, Ermsby, *and* Miles.

CONSTABLE.
Nay, masters, if you were ne'er so good, you shall before the doctors to answer your misdemeanor.

30. let's hie to] *Q1*; let us to *Q2–3*.

---

19. *vouch*] assume responsibility for.
20. *countervail*] to vie with, compete with (see xiii.97).
23. *hold . . . play*] as in combat or dueling.
26. *Mas*] a contemptuous shortening of master.
32. *rumor*] clamor, outcry.

BURDEN.

What's the matter, fellow?

CONSTABLE.

Marry, sir, here's a company of rufflers that drinking in the tavern have made a great brawl, and almost kill'd the vintner.

MILES.

Salve, Doctor Burden. This lubberly lurden,
Ill-shap'd and ill-faced, disdain'd and disgraced,
What he tells unto *vobis, mentitur de nobis.*

BURDEN.

Who is the master and chief of this crew?

MILES.

Ecce asinum mundi, fugura rotundi,
Neat, sheat, and fine, as brisk as a cup of wine.

BURDEN.

What are you?

RAFE.

I am, father doctor, as a man would say, the bellwether of this company. These are my lords, and I the Prince of Wales.

CLEMENT.

Are you Edward, the king's son?

RAFE.

Sirrah Miles, bring hither the tapster that drew the wine, and I warrant when they see how soundly I have broke his head, they'll say 'twas done by no less man than a prince.

---

37. *rufflers*] bullies.

40. *Salve*] save you.

40. *lubberly lurden*] useless blockhead.

40–42. The form of the verse spoken by Miles in this scene and in Scene ix is "Skeltonic," that is, similar in style to that written by John Skelton, Poet Laureate to Henry VIII.

42. *What . . . nobis*] "Whatever he tells you, he is lying about us."

44. *Ecce . . . rotundi*] "Behold the jackass of the round-shaped world."

44. *fugura*] *figura.*

45. *Neat*] undiluted.

45. *sheat*] trim, neat, sleek (?).

47. *bellwether*] the leading sheep of a flock.

MASON.

I cannot believe that this is the Prince of Wales.

WARREN.

And why so, sir?

MASON.

For they say the prince is a brave and a wise gentleman.

WARREN.

Why, and thinkest thou, doctor, that he is not so?
Dar'st thou detract and derogate from him,
Being so lovely and so brave a youth?

ERMSBY.

Whose face, shining with many a sugar'd smile,
Bewrays that he is bred of princely race?

MILES.

And yet, Master Doctor,   to speak like a proctor,
And tell unto you   what is veriment and true,
To cease of this quarrel,   look but on his apparel;
Then mark but my talis,   he is great Prince of Walis,
The chief of our *gregis,*   and *filius regis.*
Then 'ware what is done,   for he is Henry's white son.

RAFE.

Doctors, whose doting nightcaps are not capable of my ingenious dignity, know that I am Edward Plantagenet, whom if you displease, will make a ship that shall hold all your colleges, and so carry away the Niniversity with

65. of] *Q1,3*; off *Q2*.   71. whom] *Q1–2*; who *Q3*.

---

60. *brave*] handsome (here, of dress).
63. *like a proctor*] i.e., with authority.
64. *veriment*] verily, truly.
65. *of*] off.
66. *talis*] tales; i.e., what I tell you.
66. *Walis*] Wales.
67. *gregis . . . regis*] "chief of our congregation the son of the king."
68. *white son*] an epithet of endearment.
70. *ingenious*] intellectual.
71. *ship*] an allusion to Barclay's translation (1509) of Sebastian Brant's *Ship of Fools* (1494); see line 85, below.
72. *Niniversity*] a "ninny" was a simpleton or fool.

a fair wind to the Bankside in Southwark. How say'st thou, Ned Warren, shall I not do it?

WARREN.

Yes, my good lord; and if it please your lordship, I will gather up all your old pantofles, and with the cork make you a pinnace of five hundred ton, that shall serve the turn marvelous well, my lord.

ERMSBY.

And I, my lord, will have pioners to undermine the town, that the very gardens and orchards be carried away for your summer walks.

MILES.

And I with *scientia* and great *diligentia*
Will conjure and charm to keep you from harm;
That *utrum horum mavis,* your very great *navis,*
Like Bartlet's ship, from Oxford do skip,
With colleges and schools full loaden with fools.
Quid dices ad hoc, worshipful *domine* Dawcock?

CLEMENT.

Why, hare-brain'd courtiers, are you drunk or mad,
To taunt us up with such scurrility?
Deem you us men of base and light esteem,
To bring us such a fop for Henry's son?
Call out the beadles and convey them hence,
Straight to Bocardo; let the roisters lie
Close clapp'd in bolts, until their wits be tame.

---

73. *Bankside in Southwark*] Bankside, in the Borough of Southwark, London, on the south side of the Thames, the location of the Rose, Swan, and Globe theaters.
77. *pinnace*] a small boat belonging to a ship of war.
79. *pioners*] foot soldiers used to dig trenches or clear the ground.
84. *utrum . . . mavis*] "Whichever of these you prefer."
84. *navis*] ship.
85. *Bartlet's ship*] Barclay's *Ship of Fools.*
87. *Quid . . . hoc*] "What do you say to this?"
87. *domine Dawcock*] master Fool.
90. *light*] frivolous.
93. *Bocardo*] the old north gate of Oxford, used as a prison until the eighteenth century.
93. *roisters*] rioters, loudmouths.

ERMSBY.

Why, shall we to prison, my lord?

RAFE.

What say'st, Miles, shall I honor the prison with my presence?

MILES.

No, no; out with your blades, and hamper these jades;
Have a flirt and a crash, now play revel-dash,
And teach these *sacerdos* that the Bocardos,
Like peasants and elves, are meet for themselves.

MASON.

To the prison with them, constable.

WARREN.

Well, doctors, seeing I have sported me
With laughing at these mad and merry wags,
Know that Prince Edward is at Brazen-nose,
And this, attired like the Prince of Wales,
Is Rafe, King Henry's only loved fool;
I, Earl of Sussex; and this, Ermsby,
One of the privy chamber to the king,
Who, while the prince with Friar Bacon stays,
Have revel'd it in Oxford as you see.

MASON.

My lord, pardon us; we knew not what you were;
But courtiers may make greater scapes than these.
Will't please your honor dine with me today?

WARREN.

I will, Master Doctor, and satisfy the vintner for his hurt; only I must desire you to imagine him all this forenoon the Prince of Wales.

99. play] *Q1*; *not in Q2–3.*
108. Sussex] *Collier*; Essex *Q1–3.*
111. it] *Q1*; *not in Q2–3.*

---

98. *hamper*] put down.
99. *flirt*] a quick blow or attack.
100. *sacerdos*] priests.
101. *Like . . . themselves*] i.e., are good enough for such lowborn clowns as they are.
113. *scapes*] escapades.
116. *him*] i.e., Rafe.

MASON.

I will, sir.

RAFE.

And upon that, I will lead the way; only I will have Miles go before me, because I have heard Henry say that wisdom must go before majesty. *Exeunt omnes.*

[viii]

Enter Prince Edward *with his poniard in his hand,* Lacy *and* Margaret.

EDWARD.

Lacy, thou canst not shroud thy trait'rous thoughts,
Nor cover as did Cassius all his wiles;
For Edward hath an eye that looks as far
As Lynceus from the shores of Grecia.
Did not I sit in Oxford by the friar,
And see thee court the maid of Fressingfield,
Sealing thy flattering fancies with a kiss?
Did not proud Bungay draw his portace forth
And, joining hand in hand, had married you,
If Friar Bacon had not stroke him dumb
And mounted him upon a spirit's back,
That we might chat at Oxford with the friar?
Traitor, what answer'st? Is not all this true?

LACY.

Truth all, my lord, and thus I make reply.
At Harleston Fair, there courting for your grace,
When as mine eye survey'd her curious shape,
And drew the beauteous glory of her looks

[Scene viii]
10. stroke] *Q1*; strook *Q2–3*.

[Scene viii]

2. *cover . . . wiles*] referring to Cassius' skill in hiding the conspiracy against Caesar.

4. *Lynceus*] in Greek mythology, one of the Argonauts, whose eyesight was so keen he could see through the earth.

10. *stroke*] struck.

To dive into the center of my heart,
Love taught me that your honor did but jest,
That princes were in fancy but as men,
How that the lovely maid of Fressingfield
Was fitter to be Lacy's wedded wife
Than concubine unto the Prince of Wales.

EDWARD.

Injurious Lacy, did I love thee more
Than Alexander his Hephestion?
Did I unfold the passion of my love
And lock them in the closet of thy thoughts?
Wert thou to Edward second to himself,
Sole friend, and partner of his secret loves?
And could a glance of fading beauty break
Th' enchained fetters of such private friends?
Base coward, false, and too effeminate
To be corrival with a prince in thoughts!
From Oxford have I posted since I din'd
To quite a traitor 'fore that Edward sleep.

MARGARET.

'Twas I, my lord, not Lacy stepp'd awry;
For oft he sued and courted for yourself,
And still woo'd for the courtier all in green;
But I, whom fancy made but over-fond,
Pleaded myself with looks as if I lov'd.
I fed mine eye with gazing on his face,
And, still bewitch'd, lov'd Lacy with my looks.
My heart with sighs, mine eyes pleaded with tears,
My face held pity and content at once,

20. were in] *Q1–2*; were but in *Q3*.
26. passion] *Q1*; passions] *Q2–3*.
31. Th' enchained] *Q1–3* (Theinchained), *indicating elision*; The enchained *most eds.*
39. whom] *Q1–2*; who *Q3*.

25. *Hephestion*] in mourning for whom Alexander the Great forbade all music, pulled down the walls of cities, and in his next campaign showed no mercy to women or children.

30. *fading beauty*] i.e., beauty that will fade eventually.

32. *effeminate*] self-indulgent, yielding, unmanly.

38. *still*] continually.

And more I could not cipher out by signs
But that I lov'd Lord Lacy with my heart.
Then, worthy Edward, measure with thy mind
If women's favors will not force men fall,
If beauty and if darts of piercing love
Is not of force to bury thoughts of friends.

EDWARD.

I tell thee, Peggy, I will have thy loves.
Edward or none shall conquer Margaret.
In frigates bottom'd with rich Sethin planks,
Topp'd with the lofty firs of Lebanon,
Stemm'd and incas'd with burnish'd ivory,
And overlaid with plates of Persian wealth,
Like Thetis shalt thou wanton on the waves,
And draw the dolphins to thy lovely eyes,
To dance lavoltas in the purple streams.
Sirens, with harps and silver psalteries,
Shall wait with music at thy frigate's stem
And entertain fair Margaret with their lays.
England and England's wealth shall wait on thee;
Britain shall bend unto her prince's love
And do due homage to thine excellence,
If thou wilt be but Edward's Margaret.

MARGARET.

Pardon, my lord. If Jove's great royalty
Sent me such presents as to Danaë,

49. and if darts] *Q1–2*; and darts *Q3*
53. Sethin] *Q1–2*; Sething *Q3*.
62. their] *Collier*; her *Q1–3*.

---

45. *cipher . . . signs*] express with looks or gestures.
48. *fall*] to fall.
53. *Sethin*] Sythian (?).
57. *Thetis*] a beautiful sea-nymph.
57. *wanton*] play.
59. *lavoltas*] a courtly dance, containing many elaborate steps and turns.
60. *psalteries*] ancient stringed instruments resembling the dulcimer.
67–68. *Jove's . . . Danaë*] Jove visited Danaë, imprisoned in a tower, in a shower of gold.

If Phoebus, 'tired in Latona's weeds,
Come courting from the beauty of his lodge,
The dulcet tunes of frolic Mercury,
Not all the wealth heaven's treasury affords,
Should make me leave Lord Lacy or his love.

EDWARD.

I have learn'd at Oxford, then, this point of schools:
Ablata causa, tollitur effectus.
Lacy, the cause that Margaret cannot love
Nor fix her liking on the English prince,
Take him away, and then the effects will fail.
Villain, prepare thyself; for I will bathe
My poinard in the bosom of an earl.

LACY.

Rather than live and miss fair Margaret's love,
Prince Edward, stop not at the fatal doom,
But stab it home; end both my loves and life.

MARGARET.

Brave Prince of Wales, honored for royal deeds,
'Twere sin to stain fair Venus' courts with blood.
Love's conquests ends, my lord, in courtesy;
Spare Lacy, gentle Edward; let me die,
For so both you and he do cease your loves.

EDWARD.

Lacy shall die as traitor to his lord.

69. 'tired] *Dyce*; tied *Q1–2*; try *Q3*.
69. weeds] *this edn., after suggestion of Alfred B. Harbage*; webs *Q1–3*
71. tunes] *Q1–2*; turns *Q3*.
78. will fail] *Q1–2*; well faire *Q3*.
86. conquests] *Q1*; conquest *Q2–3*.

---

69. *Latona*] Phoebus (Apollo) and Artemis (Diana) were the twin children of Zeus and Latona.

70. *Come*] having come.

74. *point of schools*] argument in the disputations of the schools.

75. "Remove the cause, and the effect is taken away."

82–83. *stop not . . . home*] i.e., do not stop with simple sentencing, but carry it out.

82. *fatal*] fated, inevitable.

88. *cease your loves*] end your passions.

LACY.

I have deserved it; Edward, act it well.

MARGARET.

What hopes the prince to gain by Lacy's death?

EDWARD.

To end the loves 'twixt him and Margaret.

MARGARET.

Why, thinks King Henry's son that Margaret's love
Hangs in the uncertain balance of proud time,
That death shall make a discord of our thoughts?
No; stab the earl, and 'fore the morning sun
Shall vaunt him thrice over the lofty east,
Margaret will meet her Lacy in the heavens.

LACY.

If aught betides to lovely Margaret
That wrongs or wrings her honor from content,
Europe's rich wealth nor England's monarchy
Should not allure Lacy to overlive.
Then, Edward, short my life and end her loves.

MARGARET.

Rid me, and keep a friend worth many loves.

LACY.

Nay, Edward, keep a love worth many friends.

MARGARET.

And if thy mind be such as fame hath blaz'd,
Then, princely Edward, let us both abide
The fatal resolution of thy rage;
Banish thou fancy and embrace revenge,
And in one tomb knit both our carcasses,
Whose hearts were linked in one perfect love.

EDWARD [*aside*].

Edward, art thou that famous Prince of Wales
Who at Damasco beat the Saracens,
And brought'st home triumph on thy lance's point,

101. wealth] *Q1–2*; health *Q3*. 114. brought'st] *Q1–2*; brought *Q3*.

---

97. *him*] himself.
103. *short*] shorten, cut short.
104. *Rid*] destroy.
106. *blaz'd*] proclaimed.
107. *abide*] undergo, suffer.

And shall thy plumes be pull'd by Venus down?
Is it princely to dissever lovers' leagues,
To part such friends as glory in their loves?
Leave, Ned, and make a virtue of this fault,
And further Peg and Lacy in their loves.
So in subduing fancy's passion,
Conquering thyself, thou get'st the richest spoil.—
Lacy, rise up. Fair Peggy, here's my hand.
The Prince of Wales hath conquered all his thoughts,
And all his loves he yields unto the earl.
Lacy, enjoy the maid of Fressingfield;
Make her thy Lincoln countess at the church,
And Ned, as he is true Plantagenet,
Will give her to thee frankly for thy wife.

LACY.

Humbly I take her of my sovereign,
As if that Edward gave me England's right,
And rich'd me with the Albion diadem.

MARGARET.

And doth the English prince mean true?
Will he vouchsafe to cease his former loves,
And yield the title of a country maid
Unto Lord Lacy?

EDWARD.

I will, fair Peggy, as I am true lord.

MARGARET.

Then, lordly sir, whose conquest is as great,
In conquering love, as Caesar's victories,
Margaret, as mild and humble in her thoughts
As was Aspasia unto Cyrus' self,
Yields thanks, and, next Lord Lacy, doth enshrine
Edward the second secret in her heart.

116. Is it] *Q1*; Is 't *Q2–3*.
116. leagues] *Q1*; loves *Q2–3*.
117.] *not in Q2–3*.
131. rich'd] *Q1–2*; rich *Q3*.

---

140. *Aspasia*] to whom Cyrus became devoted because of her courageous modesty in the midst of a riotous feast.

142. *second secret*] next closest.

EDWARD.

Gramercy, Peggy. Now that vows are pass'd,
And that your loves are not to be revolt,
Once, Lacy, friends again, come, we will post
To Oxford; for this day the king is there,
And brings for Edward Castile Eleanor.
Peggy, I must go see and view my wife;
I pray God I like her as I loved thee.
Beside, Lord Lincoln, we shall hear dispute
'Twixt Friar Bacon and learned Vandermast.
Peggy, we'll leave you for a week or two.

MARGARET.

As it please Lord Lacy; but love's foolish looks
Think footsteps miles and minutes to be hours.

LACY.

I'll hasten, Peggy, to make short return.
But, please your honor, go unto the lodge;
We shall have butter, cheese, and venison;
And yesterday I brought for Margaret
A lusty bottle of neat claret wine.
Thus can we feast and entertain your grace.

EDWARD.

'Tis cheer, Lord Lacy, for an emperor,
If he respect the person and the place.
Come, let us in; for I will all this night
Ride post until I come to Bacon's cell. *Exeunt.*

[ix]

Enter Henry, Emperor, [Duke of Saxony,] Castile, Eleanor, Vandermast, Bungay, [*other lords and attendants*].

EMPEROR.

Trust me, Plantagenet, these Oxford schools
Are richly seated near the river side;

143. pass'd] *Schelling, Baskervill;* past *Q1–3.*
144. not to be] *Q2–3;* not be *Q1.*
[Scene ix]
0.1. *Duke of Saxony*] *Collins; not in Q1–3.*

143. *pass'd*] exchanged.
144. *revolt*] overthrown.

The mountains full of fat and fallow deer,
The battling pastures laid with kine and flocks,
The town gorgeous with high-built colleges,
And scholars seemly in their grave attire,
Learned in searching principles of art.
What is thy judgment, Jaques Vandermast?

VANDERMAST.

That lordly are the buildings of the town,
Spacious the rooms and full of pleasant walks;
But for the doctors, how that they be learned,
It may be meanly, for aught I can hear.

BUNGAY.

I tell thee, German, Hapsburg holds none such,
None read so deep as Oxenford contains.
There are within our academic state
Men that may lecture it in Germany
To all the doctors of your Belgic schools.

HENRY.

Stand to him, Bungay. Charm this Vandermast,
And I will use thee as a royal king.

VANDERMAST.

Wherein darest thou dispute with me?

BUNGAY.

In what a doctor and a friar can.

VANDERMAST.

Before rich Europe's worthies put thou forth
The doubtful question unto Vandermast.

7. searching principles] *Q1–2*; searching the principles *Q3*.

---

4. *battling*] nourishing, rich.
7. *searching*] searching out.
10. *rooms*] in the sense of areas, open places.
14. *read*] the past participle (1594 quarto spelling, "red").
14. *Oxenford*] the old form of the name.
18. *Charm*] overcome by magic.
21. *In what . . . can*] i.e., in that which a scholar and a churchman is skilled.
23. *doubtful*] difficult, perplexing.

BUNGAY.

Let it be this: whether the spirits of pyromancy or geomancy be most predominant in magic?

VANDERMAST.

I say, of pyromancy.

BUNGAY.

And I, of geomancy.

VANDERMAST.

The cabalists that write of magic spells,
As Hermes, Melchie, and Pythagoras,
Affirm that 'mongst the quadruplicity
Of elemental essence, *terra* is but thought
To be a *punctum* squared to the rest;
And that the compass of ascending elements
Exceed in bigness as they do in height;
Judging the concave circle of the sun
To hold the rest in his circumference.
If, then, as Hermes says, the fire be great'st,
Purest, and only giveth shapes to spirits,
Then must these demones that haunt that place
Be every way superior to the rest.

BUNGAY.

I reason not of elemental shapes,
Nor tell I of the concave latitudes,
Noting their essence nor their quality,
But of the spirits that pyromancy calls,

39. haunt] *Q1–2*; hunt *Q3*.

---

28. *cabalists*] writers on occult matters.

29. *Hermes, Melchie, and Pythagoras*] Hermes Trismegistus and Malchus Porphyry, neoplatonic philosophers; Pythagoras is included here because magic and mathematics were frequently connected through the mystical significance of numbers.

30–31. *'mongst . . . essence*] i.e., among the four elements (earth, air, fire, water).

31–32. *terra . . . to the rest*] i.e., earth is held to be only a spot, a point of no consequence, when measured by the others.

33. *compass*] compasses, sizes. 38. *only*] it only.

39. *demones*] spirits (the word here is trisyllabic).

39. *that place*] the sun, the place of fire.

44. *calls*] can summon.

And of the vigor of the geomantic fiends.
I tell thee, German, magic haunts the grounds,
And those strange necromantic spells,
That work such shows and wondering in the world,
Are acted by those geomantic spirits
That Hermes calleth *terrae filii.*
The fiery spirits are but transparent shades
That lightly pass as heralds to bear news;
But earthly fiends, clos'd in the lowest deep,
Dissever mountains, if they be but charg'd,
Being more gross and massy in their power.

VANDERMAST.

Rather these earthly geomantic spirits
Are dull and like the place where they remain;
For, when proud Lucifer fell from the heavens,
The spirits and angels that did sin with him
Retain'd their local essence as their faults,
All subject under Luna's continent.
They which offended less hang in the fire,
And second faults did rest within the air;
But Lucifer and his proud-hearted fiends
Were thrown into the center of the earth,
Having less understanding than the rest,
As having greater sin and lesser grace.
Therefore such gross and earthly spirits do serve
For jugglers, witches, and vild sorcerers;
Whereas the pyromantic genii

49. spirits] *Q1,3*; sprites *Q2.* 61. subject] *Q1*; subjects *Q2–3.*

---

46. *grounds*] the plural may indicate various types of earth or soils.
48. *shows*] sights. 50. *terrae filii*] "sons of the earth."
55. *gross and massy*] massive, strong.
60. *local essence*] i.e., the essence, or defining characteristic, of their localization—earth, air, and so forth.
61. *subject*] subjected.
61. *Luna's continent*] the sky; according to the Ptolemaic system, the sphere of the moon was closest to the earth.
66. *understanding*] reason.
69. *vild*] vile, common, vulgar.

Are mighty, swift, and of far-reaching power.
But grant that geomancy hath most force;
Bungay, to please these mighty potentates,
Prove by some instance what thy art can do.

BUNGAY.

I will.

EMPEROR.

Now, English Harry, here begins the game;
We shall see sport between these learned men.

VANDERMAST.

What wilt thou do?

BUNGAY.

Show thee the tree leav'd with refined gold,
Whereon the fearful dragon held his seat,
That watch'd the garden call'd Hesperides,
Subdued and won by conquering Hercules.

VANDERMAST.

Well done.

Here Bungay *conjures, and the tree appears with the dragon shooting fire.*

HENRY.

What say you, royal lordings, to my friar?
Hath he not done a point of cunning skill?

VANDERMAST.

Each scholar in the nicromantic spells
Can do as much as Bungay hath perform'd.
But as Alcmena's bastard raz'd this tree,
So will I raise him up as when he lived,
And cause him pull the dragon from his seat,
And tear the branches piecemeal from the root.

71. of] *Q1–2*; a *Q3*. 84. lordings] *Q1*; lordlings *Q2–3*.

---

80. *fearful*] i.e., to be feared. 81. *watch'd*] guarded.

83. *Well done*] (that is, if you can do it).

83.1–2. Especially considering the earthly residence of Bungay's fiends, the property tree probably appeared through the stage trap door.

88. *Alcmena's bastard*] Hercules. 91. *root*] trunk.

Hercules, *prodi, prodi,* Hercules!

Hercules *appears in his lion's skin.*

HERCULES.

Quis me vult?

VANDERMAST.

Jove's bastard son, thou Libyan Hercules,
Pull off the sprigs from off the Hesperian tree,
As once thou didst to win the golden fruit.

HERCULES.

Fiat.

Here he begins to break the branches.

VANDERMAST.

Now, Bungay, if thou canst by magic charm
The fiend appearing like great Hercules
From pulling down the branches of the tree,
Then art thou worthy to be counted learned.

BUNGAY.

I cannot.

VANDERMAST.

Cease, Hercules, until I give thee charge.
Mighty commander of this English isle,
Henry, come from the stout Plantagenets,
Bungay is learned enough to be a friar,
But to compare with Jacques Vandermast,
Oxford and Cambridge must go seek their cells
To find a man to match him in his art.
I have given nonplus to the Paduans,
To them of Sien, Florence, and Bologna,
Reimes, Louvain, and fair Rotherdam,

---

92. *prodi*] "come forth."
93. *Quis . . . vult*] "who wishes me?"
97. *Fiat*] "let it be done."
110. *given nonplus*] perplexed, discomfited.
111. *Sien*] Sienna.
112. *Reimes*] Rheims (the 1594 quarto spelling may indicate pronunciation).

Frankford, Utrech, and Orleans;
And now must Henry, if he do me right,
Crown me with laurel, as they all have done.

Enter Bacon.

BACON.
All hail to this royal company,
That sit to hear and see this strange dispute.
Bungay, how stand'st thou as a man amaz'd?
What, hath the German acted more than thou?

VANDERMAST.
What art thou that questions thus?

BACON.
Men call me Bacon.

VANDERMAST.
Lordly thou lookest, as if that thou wert learn'd;
Thy countenance, as if science held her seat
Between the circled arches of thy brows.

HENRY.
Now, monarchs, hath the German found his match.

EMPEROR.
Bestir thee, Jacques, take not now the foil,
Lest thou dost lose what foretime thou didst gain.

VANDERMAST.
Bacon, wilt thou dispute?

BACON.
No, unless he were more learn'd than Vandermast;
For yet, tell me; what hast thou done?

VANDERMAST.
Rais'd Hercules to ruinate that tree
That Bungay mounted by his magic spells.

BACON.
Set Hercules to work.

113. Utrech] *Collier*; Lutrech *Q1–3*. 120. questions] *Q1*; question'st *Q2–3*.

---

113. *Utrech*] Utrecht (?); see textual note.
117. *That sit . . . see*] (an implicit stage direction).
119. *acted*] performed.
126. *Bestir thee*] take care.
126. *foil*] defeat, fall (as in wrestling).

VANDERMAST.

Now, Hercules, I charge thee to thy task.
Pull off the golden branches from the root.

HERCULES.

I dare not. Seest thou not great Bacon here,
Whose frown doth act more than thy magic can?

VANDERMAST.

By all the thrones and dominations,
Virtues, powers, and mighty hierarchies,
I charge thee to obey to Vandermast.

HERCULES.

Bacon, that bridles headstrong Belcephon,
And rules Asmenoth, guider of the north,
Binds me from yielding unto Vandermast.

HENRY.

How now, Vandermast, have you met with your match?

VANDERMAST.

Never before was't known to Vandermast
That men held devils in such obedient awe.
Bacon doth more than art, or else I fail.

EMPEROR.

Why, Vandermast, art thou overcome?
Bacon, dispute with him and try his skill.

BACON.

I come not, monarchs, for to hold dispute
With such a novice as is Vandermast.
I come to have your royalties to dine
With Friar Bacon here in Brazen-nose;
And for this German troubles but the place,
And holds this audience with a long suspense,
I'll send him to his academy hence.
Thou, Hercules, whom Vandermast did raise,
Transport the German unto Hapsburg straight,

138–139. *thrones . . . hierarchies*] occult terms ordering the devils of varying powers.

142. *Asmenoth*] (xi.106, Astmeroth) a demon characterized by his abilities to increase a man's ability in the liberal sciences.

147. *more than art*] beyond science.

That he may learn by travail, 'gainst the spring,
More secret dooms and aphorisms of art.
Vanish the tree and thou away with him.

Exit the spirit with Vandermast *and the tree.*

EMPEROR.

Why, Bacon, whither dost thou send him?

BACON.

To Hapsburg; there your highness at return
Shall find the German in his study safe.

HENRY.

Bacon, thou hast honored England with thy skill,
And made fair Oxford famous by thine art;
I will be English Henry to thyself.
But tell me, shall we dine with thee today?

BACON.

With me, my lord; and while I fit my cheer,
See where Prince Edward comes to welcome you,
Gracious as the morning star of heaven. *Exit.*

Enter Edward, Lacy, Warren, Ermsby.

EMPEROR.

Is this Prince Edward, Henry's royal son?
How martial is the figure of his face,
Yet lovely and beset with amorets.

HENRY.

Ned, where hast thou been?

EDWARD.

At Framingham, my lord, to try your bucks
If they could 'scape the teasers or the toil;

159. travail] *Q1*; travell *Q2–3*.
159. spring] *Collier*; springs *Q1–3*.
162. whither] *Q2–3*; whether *Q1*.
177. the teasers] *Q2–3*; they teasers *Q1*.

159. *travail*] a pun: labor, travel.
160. *secret dooms*] hidden rules or judgments.
169. *cheer*] food and drink.
173. *figure*] features, physiognomy.
174. *lovely*] full of love.
174. *amorets*] looks provoking love.
177. *toil*] a large net into which the game was driven, or to narrow its path of escape.

But hearing of these lordly potentates
Landed and progress'd up to Oxford town,
I posted to give entertain to them—
Chief, to the Almain monarch; next to him,
And joint with him, Castile and Saxony,
Are welcome as they may be to the English court.
Thus for the men. But see, Venus appears,
Or one that over-matcheth Venus in her shape.
Sweet Eleanor, beauty's high-swelling pride,
Rich nature's glory and her wealth at once,
Fair of all fairs, welcome to Albion;
Welcome to me, and welcome to thine own,
If that thou deign'st the welcome from myself.

ELEANOR.

Martial Plantagenet, Henry's high-minded son,
The mark that Eleanor did count her aim,
I lik'd thee 'fore I saw thee; now, I love,
And so as in so short a time I may;
Yet so as time shall never break that so,
And therefore so accept of Eleanor.

CASTILE.

Fear not, my lord, this couple will agree,
If love may creep into their wanton eyes;
And therefore, Edward, I accept thee here,
Without suspense as my adopted son.

HENRY.

Let me that joy in these consorting greets,
And glory in these honors done to Ned,
Yield thanks for all these favors to my son,

203. these] *Q1–2*; those *Q3*.

---

180. *entertain*] entertainment.
182. *joint*] joined, equally.
184. *Thus*] so much.
188. *fairs*] fair women.
194–195. *And so . . . that so*] i.e., "I love you as much as I am able in so short a time, but that is so greatly that time shall never diminish it."
201. *joy*] rejoice.
201. *consorting greets*] harmonious greetings, compliments.

And rest a true Plantagenet to all.

Enter Miles *with a cloth and trenchers and salt.*

MILES.

Salvete, omnes reges, that govern your *greges,*
In Saxony and Spain, in England and in Almain;
For all this frolic rable must I cover thee, table,
With trenchers, salt, and cloth, and then look for your broth.

EMPEROR.

What pleasant fellow is this?

HENRY.

'Tis, my lord, Doctor Bacon's poor scholar.

MILES [*aside*].

My master hath made me sewer of these great lords, and God knows I am as serviceable at a table as a sow is under an apple tree. 'Tis no matter; their cheer shall not be great, and therefore what skills where the salt stand, before or behind? [*Exit.*]

CASTILE.

These scholars knows more skill in axioms,
How to use quips and sleights of sophistry,
Than for to cover courtly for a king.

Enter Miles *with a mess of pottage and broth, and after him,* Bacon.

MILES.

Spill, sir? Why, do you think I never carried twopenny chop before in my life?

207. thee, table] *Q1*; the table *Q2–3*

216. knows] *Q1*; know *Q2–3*; axioms *Q2, Collier*; actioms *Q1, Grosart*; Axomies *Q3*.

205. *Salvete . . . reges*] "Hail, all you kings."
205. *greges*] "peoples."
207. *rable*] rabble.
211. *sewer*] the officer who set the places at a feast.
214. *what skills*] what difference does it make.
217. *sleights*] tricks, as in "sleight-of-hand."

By your leave, *nobile decus,* for here comes Doctor Bacon's *pecus,*
Being in his full age, to carry a mess of pottage.

BACON.

Lordings, admire not if your cheer be this,
For we must keep our academic fare.
No riot where philosophy doth reign;
And therefore, Henry, place these potentates,
And bid them fall unto their frugal cates.

EMPEROR.

Presumptuous friar, what, scoff'st thou at a king?
What, dost thou taunt us with thy peasants' fare,
And give us cates fit for country swains?
Henry, proceeds this jest of thy consent,
To twit us with such a pittance of such price?
Tell me, and Frederick will not grieve thee long.

HENRY.

By Henry's honor and the royal faith
The English monarch beareth to his friend,
I knew not of the friar's feeble fare;
Nor am I pleas'd he entertains you thus.

BACON.

Content thee, Frederick, for I show'd the cates
To let thee see how scholars use to feed,
How little meat refines our English wits.
Miles, take away, and let it be thy dinner.

MILES.

Marry, sir, I will. This day shall be a festival day with me,
For I shall exceed in the highest degree. *Exit* Miles.

221–222.] *Q1–3 print as prose.* 230. give] *Q1*; gives *Q2–3.*
232. with such a] *Q1*; with a *Q2–3.* 238. the cates] *Q1*; thee cates *Q2–3.*
242–243.] *Q1–3 print as prose.*

---

221. *nobile decus*] "your worshipful honor."

221. *pecus*] "beast of burden."

222. *pottage*] a thick soup, made of vegetables; the line is perhaps a comic allusion to Genesis xxv:29–34, in which Esau sells his birthright for Jacob's mess of pottage.

223. *admire not*] don't wonder.

227. *cates*] usually, delicacies; here, morsels.

239. *use to*] are accustomed to.

BACON.

I tell thee, monarch, all the German peers
Could not afford thy entertainment such,
So royal and so full of majesty,
As Bacon will present to Frederick.
The basest waiter that attends thy cups
Shall be in honors greater than thyself;
And for thy cates, rich Alexandria drugs,
Fetch'd by carvels from Egypt's richest straits,
Found in the wealthy strond of Africa,
Shall royalize the table of my king.
Wines richer than the 'Gyptian courtesan
Quaff'd to Augustus' kingly counter-match
Shall be carous'd in English Henry's feasts;
Kandy shall yield the richest of her canes;
Persia, down her Volga by canoes,
Send down the secrets of her spicery;
The Afric dates, mirabolans of Spain,
Conserves and suckets from Tiberias,
Cates from Judea, choicer than the lamp
That fired Rome with sparks of gluttony,
Shall beautify the board for Frederick;
And therefore grudge not at a friar's feast. [*Exeunt.*]

254. the 'Gyptian] *Q1*; the Gyprian *Q2–3*.
260. mirabolans] *Dyce*; mirabiles *Q1–3*.
256. feasts] *Q1–2*; feast *Q3*.

---

250. *thy*] Bacon turns to Henry on this line, indicated by "my king," l. 253.

250. *drugs*] spices.

251. *carvels*] caravels, a light Portuguese sailing ship.

254. *'Gyptian courtesan*] Cleopatra.

255. *Augustus' kingly counter-match*] Antony.

256. *carous'd*] drunk in festivity. 257. *Kandy*] in Ceylon.

260. *mirabolans*] dried plums. 261. *suckets*] sweetmeats.

261. *Tiberias*] Galilee.

262–263. *lamp . . . gluttony*] an obscure allusion; lamprey eel (?), sometimes included in more decadent Roman menus (see Juvenal *Sat.* IV).

[x]

Enter two gentlemen, Lambert *and* Serlsby, *with the* keeper.

LAMBERT.

Come, frolic keeper of our liege's game,
Whose table spread hath ever venison
And jacks of wine to welcome passengers,
Know I am in love with jolly Margaret,
That over-shines our damsels as the moon
Dark'neth the brightest sparkles of the night.
In Laxfield here my land and living lies;
I'll make thy daughter jointer of it all,
So thou consent to give her to my wife;
And I can spend five hundred marks a year.

SERLSBY.

I am the lands-lord, keeper, of thy holds;
By copy all thy living lies in me;
Laxfield did never see me raise my due.
I will enfeoff fair Margaret in all,
So she will take her to a lusty squire.

KEEPER.

Now, courteous gentles, if the keeper's girl
Hath pleased the liking fancy of you both,
And with her beauty hath subdued your thoughts,
'Tis doubtful to decide the question.
It joys me that such men of great esteem
Should lay their liking on this base estate,
And that her state should grow so fortunate

14. fair] *Q1; not in Q2–3.*

---

3. *jacks*] pitchers or jugs.
7. *Laxfield*] northeast of Framlingham.
8. *jointer*] person on whom an estate is settled.
9. *to my wife*] for my wife.
11. *holds*] holdings, property.
12. *By copy*] by copyhold tenure, by which the tenant was given a copy of the tenure agreement concerning his land, by the manorial court, but had no other proof of right of residence.
13. *due*] rents.
14. *enfeoff*] to write over in possession, to hand over entirely.
19. *doubtful*] difficult.

To be a wife to meaner men than you.
But sith such squires will stoop to keeper's fee,
I will, to avoid displeasure of you both,
Call Margaret forth, and she shall make her choice. *Exit.*

LAMBERT.

Content, keeper, send her unto us.
Why, Serlsby, is thy wife so lately dead,
Are all thy loves so lightly passed over,
As thou canst wed before the year be out?

SERLSBY.

I live not, Lambert, to content the dead;
Nor was I wedded but for life to her.
The grave ends and begins a married state.

Enter Margaret.

LAMBERT.

Peggy, the lovely flower of all towns,
Suffolk's fair Helen and rich England's star,
Whose beauty tempered with her huswifery
Makes England talk of merry Fressingfield!

SERLSBY.

I cannot trick it up with poesies,
Nor paint my passions with comparisons,
Nor tell a tale of Phoebus and his loves;
But this believe me: Laxfield here is mine,
Of ancient rent seven hundred pounds a year,
And, if thou canst but love a country squire,
I will enfeoff thee, Margaret, in all.
I cannot flatter; try me, if thou please.

MARGARET.

Brave neighboring squires, the stay of Suffolk's clime,
A keeper's daughter is too base in 'gree

25. to avoid] *Q1*; t'avoid *Q2–3*.
33. grave] *Q2–3*; graves *Q1*.
47. daughter] *Q2–3*; daughters *Q1*.

24. *sith*] since.
24. *fee*] income, social station.
38. *trick it up with poesies*] decorate my expression poetically.
39. *comparisons*] similes and metaphors.
42. *ancient*] long-established.
46. *stay*] support.
46. *clime*] region, country.
47. *'gree*] degree.

To match with men accompted of such worth.
But might I not displease, I would reply.

LAMBERT.

Say, Peggy. Naught shall make us discontent.

MARGARET.

Then, gentles, note that love hath little stay,
Nor can the flames that Venus sets on fire
Be kindled but by fancy's motion.
Then pardon, gentles, if a maid's reply
Be doubtful, while I have debated with myself,
Who or of whom love shall constrain me like.

SERLSBY.

Let it be me; and trust me, Margaret,
The meads environed with the silver streams,
Whose battling pastures fatt'neth all my flocks,
Yielding forth fleeces stapled with such wool
As Lempster cannot yield more finer stuff,
And forty kine with fair and burnish'd heads,
With strouting dugs that paggle to the ground,
Shall serve thy dairy if thou wed with me.

LAMBERT.

Let pass the country wealth, as flocks and kine,
And lands that wave with Ceres' golden sheaves,
Filling my barns with plenty of the fields;
But, Peggy, if thou wed thyself to me,
Thou shalt have garments of embroder'd silk,
Lawns, and rich networks for thy head-attire.

48. accompted] *Q1*; accounted *Q2–3*.
52. sets] *Q1–2*; set *Q3*.
59. fatt'neth] *Q1*; fatten *Q2–3*.
63. paggle] *Q1*; puggle *Q2–3*.

---

48. *accompted*] accounted.
51. *stay*] sobriety, stability.
60. *stapled*] fibered; the staple in wool, its fibrous content, was judged by its fineness.
61. *Lempster*] Leominster, in Herefordshire.
62. *burnish'd*] golden, gleaming. 63. *strouting*] bulging, swelling.
63. *paggle*] hang loosely (unique example of the word in English).
66. *Ceres*] the deity of the generative powers of nature.
69. *embroder'd*] embroidered.
70. *Lawns*] a variety of very fine linen.

Costly shall be thy fair 'abiliments,
If thou wilt be but Lambert's loving wife.

MARGARET.

Content you, gentles. You have proffered fair,
And more than fits a country maid's degree.
But give me leave to counsel me a time;
For fancy blooms not at the first assault.
Give me but ten days respite and I will reply
Which or to whom myself affectionates.

SERLSBY.

Lambert, I tell thee thou art importunate;
Such beauty fits not such a base esquire.
It is for Serlsby to have Margaret.

LAMBERT.

Think'st thou with wealth to over-reach me?
Serlbsy, I scorn to brook thy country braves.
I dare thee, coward, to maintain this wrong
At dint of rapier, single in the field.

SERLSBY.

I'll answer, Lambert, what I have avouch'd.
Margaret, farewell; another time shall serve. *Exit* Serlsby.

LAMBERT.

I'll follow. Peggy, farewell to thyself;
Listen how well I'll answer for thy love. *Exit* Lambert.

MARGARET.

How Fortune tempers lucky haps with frowns,
And wrongs me with the sweets of my delight.
Love is my bliss; and love is now my bale.

71. 'abiliments] *Q1*; habiliments *Q2–3*
82–83. me?/ Serlsby,] *Collier*; me/ Serlsby, *Q1*; me/ Serlsby? *Q2–3*.
80. a base] *Q1–2*; *not in Q3*.
89. Listen] *Q1–2*; List *Q3*.

---

71. *'abiliments*] habiliments; perhaps both Greene and his actors dropped their *H*'s.

75. *to counsel me*] to take counsel with myself.

78. *myself affectionates*] I feel affection.

83. *braves*] boasts.

85. *At dint*] by means of attack or blows.

90. *haps*] events.

Shall I be Helen in my froward fates,
As I am Helen in my matchless hue,
And set rich Suffolk with my face afire?
If lovely Lacy were but with his Peggy,
The cloudy darkness of his bitter frown
Would check the pride of these aspiring squires.
Before the term of ten days be expired,
When as they look for answer of their loves,
My lord will come to merry Fressingfield
And end their fancies and their follies both;
Till when, Peggy, be blithe and of good cheer.

Enter a post *with a letter and a bag of gold.*

POST.

Fair lovely damsel, which way leads this path?
How might I post me unto Fressingfield?
Which footpath leadeth to the keeper's lodge?

MARGARET.

Your way is ready and this path is right.
Myself do dwell hereby in Fressingfield,
And, if the keeper be the man you seek,
I am his daughter. May I know the cause?

POST.

Lovely and once beloved of my lord—
No marvel if his eye was lodg'd so low,
When brighter beauty is not in the heavens—
The Lincoln earl hath sent you letters here,
And with them, just an hundred pounds in gold.
Sweet bonny wench, read them and make reply.

MARGARET.

The scrolls that Jove sent Danaë,
Wrapp'd in rich closures of fine burnish'd gold,
Were not more welcome than these lines to me.

93. froward] *Collier*; forward *Q1–3*. 105. me] *Q1–2; not in Q3*.
108. hereby] *Q1–2*; hard by *Q3*. 113. brighter] *Q1–2*; bright *Q3*.

---

107. *ready*] close at hand. 115. *just*] exactly.
118. *burnish'd*] highly polished.

Tell me, whilst that I do unrip the seals,
Lives Lacy well? How fares my lovely lord?

POST.

Well, if that wealth may make men to live well.

The letter, and Margaret reads it.

"The blooms of the almond tree grow in a night, and vanish in a morn; the flies *haemerae,* fair Peggy, take life with the sun, and die with the dew; fancy, that slippeth in with a gaze, goeth out with a wink; and too timely loves have ever the shortest length. I write this as thy grief, and my folly, who at Fressingfield lov'd that which time hath taught me to be but mean dainties. Eyes are dissemblers, and fancy is but queasy. Therefore know, Margaret, I have chosen a Spanish lady to be my wife, chief waiting-woman to the Princess Eleanor: a lady fair, and no less fair than thyself, honorable and wealthy. In that I forsake thee, I leave thee to thine own liking; and for thy dowry I have sent thee an hundred pounds, and ever assure thee of my favor, which shall avail thee and thine much. Farewell.

Not thine nor his own,

Edward Lacy"

Fond Ate, doomer of bad-boding fates,
That wraps proud Fortune in thy snaky locks,

131. chosen] *Q1–2*; chose *Q3*.
134. forsake] *Q1–2*; forsooke *Q3*.
140. bad-boding] *Q1*; bad boasting *Q2–3*.

122.1. *The letter*] This formal device (its traditional nature preserved even in the typography of the quartos) occurs again and again in Greene's novels; as in these works, its style is euphuistic; note, however, that this letter is planned for a theatrically appropriate length, for stage reading.

123–124. *blooms . . . morn*] a doubtful piece of natural lore; perhaps incorrectly remembered from Pliny *Nat. Hist.* XIII.xvii.60–62, perhaps invented by Greene.

124. *haemerae*] ephemera, an insect that lives only for a day.

126–127. *too timely loves*] too hasty passions.

130. *fancy . . . queasy*] passion is nothing if not fickle.

140. *Ate*] goddess of catastrophe and mischief; "fond" here signifies her capricious cruelty, ordinarily associated with Fortune herself.

140. *doomer*] controller, judge.

Didst thou enchant my birthday with such stars
As lighten'd mischief from their infancy?
If heavens had vow'd, if stars had made decree,
To show on me their froward influence,
If Lacy had but lov'd, heavens, hell, and all,
Could not have wrong'd the patience of my mind.

POST.
It grieves me, damsel, but the earl is forc'd
To love the lady by the king's command.

MARGARET.
The wealth combin'd within the English shelves,
Europe's commander, nor the English king
Should not have mov'd the love of Peggy from her lord.

POST.
What answer shall I return to my lord?

MARGARET.
First, for thou cam'st from Lacy, whom I lov'd—
Ah, give me leave to sigh at every thought!—
Take thou, my friend, the hundred pound he sent;
For Margaret's resolution craves no dower.
The world shall be to her as vanity;
Wealth, trash; love, hate; pleasure, despair.
For I will straight to stately Framingham,
And in the abbey there be shorn a nun,
And yield my loves and liberty to God.
Fellow, I give thee this, not for the news,
For those be hateful unto Margaret,
But for th'art Lacy's man, once Margaret's love.

POST.
What I have heard, what passions I have seen,
I'll make report of them unto the earl. *Exit* Post.

MARGARET.
Say that she joys his fancies be at rest,

145. on] *Q1*; in *Q2–3*.

---

145. *froward influence*] hostile influence, in the astrological sense.
150. *shelves*] cliffs.
166. *passions*] here, speeches of sorrow and emotional intensity.

And prays that his misfortune may be hers. *Exit.*

[xi]

Enter Friar Bacon *drawing the curtains with a white stick, a book in his hand, and a lamp lighted by him, and the* brazen head; *and* Miles, *with weapons by him.*

BACON.

Miles, where are you?

MILES.

Here, sir.

BACON.

How chance you tarry so long?

MILES.

Think you that the watching of the brazen head craves no furniture? I warrant you, sir, I have so armed myself that if all your devils come I will not fear them an inch.

BACON.

Miles, thou knowest that I have dived into hell
And sought the darkest palaces of fiends;
That with my magic spells great Belcephon
Hath left his lodge and kneeled at my cell;
The rafters of the earth rent from the poles,
And three-form'd Luna hid her silver looks,
Trembling upon her concave continent,
When Bacon read upon his magic book.
With seven years' tossing nigromantic charms,

169. misfortune] *Q1*; misfortunes *Q2–3*.
8. of fiends] *Q1*; of the fiends *Q2–3*.
[Scene xi]
6. devils come] *Q1*; devils do come *Q2–3*.
15. With] *Q1–2*; When *Q3*.

[Scene xi]

0.1–3. S.D. see Appendix A.

0.1. *a white stick*] the magic wand of the professional conjurer, white for the purity required by the art.

4–5. *craves no furniture*] requires no weapons.

6. *fear . . . inch*] retreat from them in fear even a bit.

12. *three-form'd Luna*] from Ovid *Met.* VII.177, *"diva triformis,"* i.e., Luna, Diana, Hecate simultaneously.

13. *concave continent*] the sphere of the moon, the sky.

Poring upon dark Hecat's principles,
I have fram'd out a monstrous head of brass,
That, by th' enchanting forces of the devil,
Shall tell out strange and uncouth aphorisms,
And girt fair England with a wall of brass.
Bungay and I have watch'd these threescore days,
And now our vital spirits crave some rest.
If Argus liv'd, and had his hundred eyes,
They could not overwatch Phobeter's night.
Now, Miles, in thee rests Friar Bacon's weal;
The honor and renown of all his life
Hangs in the watching of this brazen head.
Therefore, I charge thee by the immortal God,
That holds the souls of men within his fist,
This night thou watch; for, ere the morning star
Sends out his glorious glister on the north,
The head will speak. Then, Miles, upon thy life,
Wake me; for then by magic art I'll work
To end my seven years' task with excellence.
If that a wink but shut thy watchful eye,
Then farewell Bacon's glory and his fame.
Draw close the curtains, Miles. Now, for thy life,
Be watchful, and— *Here he falleth asleep.*

MILES.

So. I thought you would talk yourself asleep anon; and 'tis no marvel, for Bungay on the days and he on the nights have watch'd just these ten-and-fifty days. Now this is the night, and 'tis my task and no more. Now, Jesus bless me, what a goodly head it is; and a nose! you talk of *nos autem glorificare,* but here's a nose that I warrant may be call'd *nos autem popelare* for the people of the parish. Well, I am furnished with weapons. Now, sir, I will set me down by a post, and make it as good as a

---

19. *uncouth*] mysterious, strange.
23. *Argus*] the hundred-eyed watchman of Io.
24. *Phobeter*] another name for Morpheus, god of sleep and dreams.
25. *weal*] welfare, prosperity.
47. *by a post*] next to one of the structural columns on the Elizabethan apron stage, holding up the "heavens," or the overhanging roof.

watchman to wake me if I chance to slumber. I thought, Goodman Head, I would call you out of your memento.

Sit down and knock your head.

Passion a' God, I have almost broke my pate! Up, Miles, to your task; take your brown bill in your hand; here's some of your master's hobgoblins abroad.

With this a great noise. The Head *speaks.*

HEAD.

Time is.

MILES.

Time is? Why, Master Brazen-head, have you such a capital nose, and answer you with syllables, "Time is"? Is this all my master's cunning, to spend seven years' study about "Time is"? Well, sir, it may be we shall have some better orations of it anon. Well, I'll watch you as narrowly as ever you were watch'd, and I'll play with you as the nightingale with the slowworm: I'll set a prick against my breast. [*Places the point of the halberd against his breast.*] Now, rest there, Miles. [*Falls asleep.*] Lord have mercy upon me, I have almost kill'd myself! [*Noise again.*] Up, Miles; list how they rumble.

HEAD.

Time was.

MILES.

Well, Friar Bacon, you spent your seven years' study well, that can make your head speak but two words at once. "Time was." Yea, marry, time was when my master was a wise man, but that was before he began to make the brazen head. You shall lie, while your arse ache and your

51. here's] *Q1–2*; here *Q3*.
52. master's] *Q1–2*; master *Q3*.
59. were] *Q1–2*; was *Q3*.
66. spent] *Q1*; have spent *Q2–3*.

---

49. *memento*] reverie, slumber, brown study.

49.1. *knock your head*] i.e., by falling asleep and letting it knock against the column.

51. *brown bill*] halberd.

60–61. *nightingale . . . breast*] The nightingale singing with a pricking thorn against its breast was a traditional image of religious and lyric poetry; the slowworm is the serpent.

70. *lie*] lie abed.

head speak no better. Well, I will watch, and walk up and down, and be a peripatetian and a philosopher of Aristotle's stamp. [*Noise again.*] What, a fresh noise? Take thy pistols in hand, Miles.

Here the Head *speaks; and a lightning flasheth forth, and a hand appears that breaketh down the* Head *with a hammer.*

HEAD.

Time is past.

MILES.

Master, master, up! Hell's broken loose; your head speaks, and there's such a thunder and lightning that I warrant all Oxford is up in arms. Out of your bed, and take a brown bill in your hand. The latter day is come.

BACON.

Miles, I come. Oh, passing warily watch'd;
Bacon will make thee next himself in love.
When spake the head?

MILES.

When spake the head! Did not you say that he should tell strange principles of philosophy? Why, sir, it speaks but two words at a time.

BACON.

Why, villain, hath it spoken oft?

MILES.

Oft? Ay, marry, hath it, thrice. But in all those three times it hath uttered but seven words.

BACON.

As how?

MILES.

Marry, sir, the first time he said, "Time is." As if Fabius

77. thunder] *Q1–2*; thundring *Q3*. 86. spoken] *Q1–2*; spoke *Q3*.

72–73. *peripatetian . . . Aristotle's stamp*] Aristotle would teach walking beneath the portico of the Lyceum in Athens, and his philosophical scholars were given the name of Peripatetics.

79. *latter day*] Doomsday, the day of Judgment.

81. *next himself in love*] i.e., next, after myself, in favor.

90–91. *Fabius Cumentator*] probably Q. Fabius Maximus, surnamed "Cunctator."

Cumentator should have pronounc'd a sentence, he said, "Time was." And the third time, with thunder and lightning, as in great choler, he said, "Time is past."

BACON.

'Tis past indeed. Ah, villain, time is past;
My life, my fame, my glory, all are past.
Bacon, the turrets of thy hope are ruin'd down;
Thy seven years' study lieth in the dust;
Thy brazen head lies broken through a slave
That watch'd, and would not when the head did will.
What said the head first?

MILES.

Even, sir, "Time is."

BACON.

Villain, if thou hadst call'd to Bacon then,
If thou hadst watch'd, and wak'd the sleepy friar,
The brazen head had uttered aphorisms,
And England had been circled round with brass.
But proud Astmeroth, ruler of the north,
And Demogorgon, master of the fates,
Grudge that a mortal man should work so much.
Hell trembled at my deep, commanding spells;
Fiends frown'd to see a man their over-match.
Bacon might boast more than a man might boast,
But now the braves of Bacon hath an end;
Europe's conceit of Bacon hath an end;
His seven years' practice sorteth to ill end;
And, villain, sith my glory hath an end,
I will appoint thee fatal to some end.

91. Cumentator] *Q1*; commentator *Q2–3*.

96. turrets of thy] *Q1–2*; terrours of my *Q3*.

94. Ah, villain] *Dyce*; a villaine *Q1–3*

112. hath] *Q1–2*; have *Q3*.

---

107. *Demogorgon*] first mentioned about A.D. 450; at first, the most terrible devil invoked by magic, eventually the name of a mysterious infernal diety.

111. *might boast*] was allowed to boast.

113. *conceit*] opinion.

114. *sorteth*] falls out, comes.

116. *fatal to some end*] doomed to some end.

Villain, avoid; get thee from Bacon's sight.
Vagrant, go roam and range about the world,
And perish as a vagabond on earth.

MILES.

Why then, sir, you forbid me your service.

BACON

My service, villain, with a fatal curse
That direful plagues and mischief fall on thee.

MILES.

'Tis no matter. I am against you with the old proverb, "The more the fox is curs'd, the better he fares." God be with you, sir. I'll take but a book in my hand, a wide-sleeved gown on my back, and a crowned cap on my head, and see if I can want promotion. [*Exit.*]

BACON.

Some fiend or ghost haunt on thy weary steps,
Until they do transport thee quick to hell;
For Bacon shall have never merry day,
To lose the fame and honor of his head. *Exit.*

[xii]

Enter Emperor, Castile, Henry, Eleanor, Edward, Lacy, Rafe, [*and attendants*].

EMPEROR.

Now, lovely prince, the prince of Albion's wealth,
How fares the Lady Eleanor and you?
What, have you courted and found Castile fit
To answer England in equivalence?
Will't be a match 'twixt bonny Nell and thee?

EDWARD.

Should Paris enter in the courts of Greece
And not lie fettered in fair Helen's looks?

118. range] *Q1–2*; rage *Q3*.

---

117. *avoid*] be gone, away!
118. *Vagrant*] a Latinate adjective; like a vagrant, wandering.
118. *range*] wander.
123. *I am against you*] I am beforehand with you.
124. *curs'd*] sometimes with a pun on "coursed," i.e., pursued.
126. *crowned cap*] probably resembling the scholar's academic cap.
127. *want*] lack. 129. *quick*] alive.

Or Phoebus 'scape those piercing amorets
That Daphne glanced at his deity?
Can Edward then sit by a flame and freeze,
Whose heat puts Helen and fair Daphne down?
Now, monarchs, ask the lady if we 'gree.

HENRY.

What, madam, hath my son found grace or no?

ELEANOR.

Seeing, my lord, his lovely counterfeit,
And hearing how his mind and shape agreed,
I come not, troop'd with all this warlike train,
Doubting of love, but so affectionate
As Edward hath in England what he won in Spain.

CASTILE.

A match, my lord; these wantons needs must love.
Men must have wives and women will be wed.
Let's haste the day to honor up the rites.

RAFE.

Sirrah Harry, shall Ned marry Nell?

HENRY.

Ay, Rafe; how then?

RAFE.

Marry, Harry, follow my counsel. Send for Friar Bacon to marry them, for he'll so conjure him and her with his nigromancy, that they shall love together like pig and lamb whilst they live.

CASTILE.

But hear'st thou, Rafe, art thou content to have Eleanor to thy lady?

RAFE.

Ay, so she will promise me two things.

20. will] *Q1*; must *Q2–3*.

---

11. *puts . . . down*] excels.
18. *As*] that.
26–27. *they shall . . . live*] implying that without necromancy they should never do so.

CASTILE.

What's that, Rafe?

RAFE.

That she will never scold with Ned, nor fight with me. Sirrah Harry, I have put her down with a thing unpossible.

HENRY.

What's that, Rafe?

RAFE.

Why, Harry, didst thou ever see that a woman could both hold her tongue and her hands? No. But when egg-pies grows on apple trees, then will thy gray mare prove a bagpiper.

EMPEROR.

What says the Lord of Castile and the Earl of Lincoln, that they are in such earnest and secret talk?

CASTILE.

I stand, my lord, amazed at his talk,
How he discourseth of the constancy
Of one surnam'd, for beauty's excellence,
The Fair Maid of merry Fressingfield.

HENRY.

'Tis true, my lord, 'tis wondrous for to hear;
Her beauty passing Mars's paramour,
Her virgin's right as rich as Vesta's was.
Lacy and Ned hath told me miracles.

CASTILE.

What says Lord Lacy? Shall she be his wife?

LACY.

Or else Lord Lacy is unfit to live.
May it please your highness give me leave to post
To Fressingfield, I'll fetch the bonny girl,
And prove in true appearance at the court
What I have vouched often with my tongue.

38. grows] *Q1*; grow *Q2–3*.
44. beauty's] *Q1–2*; beauteous *Q3*.
45. merry] *Q1*; *not in Q2–3*.
49. hath] *Q1*; have *Q2–3*.

40–41. *What says . . . talk*] Lacy and Castile presumably have engaged in private conversation, in pantomime.

HENRY.

Lacy, go to the querry of my stable
And take such coursers as shall fit thy turn.
Hie thee to Fressingfield and bring home the lass;
And for her fame flies through the English coast,
If it may please the Lady Eleanor,
One day shall match your excellence and her.

ELEANOR.

We Castile ladies are not very coy.
Your highness may command a greater boon;
And glad were I to grace the Lincoln earl
With being partner of his marriage day.

EDWARD.

Gramercy, Nell; for I do love the lord
As he that's second to myself in love.

RAFE.

You love her? Madam Nell, never believe him you though he swears he loves you.

ELEANOR.

Why, Rafe?

RAFE.

Why, his love is like unto a tapster's glass that is broken with every touch; for he loved the Fair Maid of Fressingfield once, out of all ho. Nay, Ned, never wink upon me; I care not, I.

HENRY.

Rafe tells all; you shall have a good secretary of him.
But Lacy, haste thee post to Fressingfield,

71. broken] *Q1–2*; broke *Q3*.

---

56. *querry*] Equerry, officer in charge of royal stables.
59. *for*] because.
61. *One day . . . her*] i.e., one day shall see your wedding and hers.
62. *coy*] here, aloof.
66–67. *for I do love . . . in love*] i.e., I love Lacy because he is in love with Margaret almost as much as I am with you.
73. *out of all ho*] beyond all bounds, all calling (similar to terms of falconry).
76. *post*] quickly

For ere thou hast fitted all things for her state,
The solemn marriage day will be at hand.

LACY.
I go, my lord. *Exit* Lacy.

EMPEROR.
How shall we pass this day, my lord?

HENRY.
To horse, my lord. The day is passing fair;
We'll fly the partridge or go rouse the deer.
Follow, my lords; you shall not want for sport. *Exeunt.*

[xiii] *Enter* Friar Bacon *with* Friar Bungay *to his cell.*

BUNGAY.
What means the friar that frolick'd it of late
To sit as melancholy in his cell
As if he had neither lost nor won today?

BACON.
Ah, Bungay, my brazen head is spoil'd,
My glory gone, my seven years' study lost.
The fame of Bacon, bruited through the world,
Shall end and perish with this deep disgrace.

BUNGAY.
Bacon hath built foundation on his fame
So surely on the wings of true report,
With acting strange and uncouth miracles,
As this cannot infringe what he deserves.

BACON.
Bungay, sit down; for by prospective skill
I find this day shall fall out ominous.
Some deadly act shall 'tide me ere I sleep,
But what and wherein little can I guess.

77. For ere] *Brooke, Baskervill*; Or ere *most eds.*; Eor ere *Q1–3*.
[Scene xiii]
2.] *Line repeated in Q1*.
10. and] *Q1–2; not in Q3*.
14. 'tide] *Q1*; betide *Q2–3*.

[Scene xiii]
3. *As if . . . today*] without direction, apathetic, confused.
6. *bruited*] reported.
8. *on*] of.
14. *'tide*] betide.

BUNGAY.

My mind is heavy, whatso'er shall hap.

Enter two Scholars, *sons to Lambert and Serlsby. Knock.*

BACON.

Who's that knocks?

BUNGAY.

Two scholars that desires to speak with you.

BACON.

Bid them come in. Now, my youths, what would you have?

1ST SCHOLAR.

Sir, we are Suffolk men and neighboring friends,
Our fathers, in their countries, lusty squires;
Their lands adjoin. In Crackfield mine doth dwell,
And his in Laxfield. We are college mates,
Sworn brothers, as our fathers lives as friends.

BACON.

To what end is all this?

2ND SCHOLAR.

Hearing your worship kept within your cell
A glass prospective wherein men might see
Whatso their thoughts or hearts' desire could wish,
We come to know how that our fathers fare.

BACON.

My glass is free for every honest man.
Sit down and you shall see ere long
How or in what state your friendly fathers lives.
Meanwhile, tell me your names.

1ST SCHOLAR.

Mine Lambert.

2ND SCHOLAR.

And mine Serlsby.

32. fathers lives] *Collins*; father lives *Q1*; fathers live *Q2–3*.

16.1. The S.D. indicates a detail of staging; the two sons walked upon the stage *before* reaching the acting area of the study, where they knock upon something—a column or wall.

22. *Crackfield*] Cratfield, a village nine miles from Framlingham.

BACON.

Bungay, I smell there will be a tragedy.

Enter Lambert *and* Serlsby, *with rapiers and daggers.*

LAMBERT.

Serlsby, thou hast kept thine hour like a man.
Th'art worthy of the title of a squire
That durst, for proof of thy affection,
And for thy mistress' favor, prize thy blood.
Thou know'st what words did pass at Fressingfield,
Such shameless braves as manhood cannot brook;
Ay, for I scorn to bear such piercing taunts,
Prepare thee, Serlsby; one of us will die.

SERLSBY.

Thou see'st I single thee the field,
And what I spake, I'll maintain with my sword.
Stand on thy guard; I cannot scold it out.
And if thou kill me, think I have a son,
That lives in Oxford, in the Broadgates Hall,
Who will revenge his father's blood with blood.

LAMBERT.

And, Serlsby, I have there a lusty boy
That dares at weapon buckle with thy son,
And lives in Broadgates too, as well as thine.
But draw thy rapier, for we'll have a bout.

BACON.

Now, lusty younkers, look within the glass,
And tell me if you can discern your sires.

46. spake] *Q1–2*; speak *Q3*.

36.1. *rapiers and daggers*] A duelist would commonly carry both weapons in fight.

40. *prize*] risk.

43. *for*] because.

45. *single thee the field*] take thee apart, draw out; based in hunting terminology, where one deer would be drawn out and separated from the others, for the chase.

49. *Broadgates Hall*] now part of Pembroke College.

52. *buckle with*] fight with, take on.

55. *younkers*] young men.

1ST SCHOLAR.

Serlsby, 'tis hard; thy father offers wrong,
To combat with my father in the field.

2ND SCHOLAR.

Lambert, thou liest; my father's is the abuse,
And thou shalt find it, if my father harm.

BUNGAY.

How goes it, sirs?

1ST SCHOLAR.

Our fathers are in combat hard by Fressingfield.

BACON.

Sit still, my friends, and see the event.

LAMBERT.

Why stand'st thou, Serlsby? Doubt'st thou of thy life?
A veney, man; fair Margaret craves so much.

SERLSBY.

Then this, for her!

1ST SCHOLAR.

Ah, well thrust.

2ND SCHOLAR.

But mark the ward.

They fight and kill each other.

LAMBERT.

Oh, I am slain!

SERLSBY.

And I; Lord have mercy on me.

1ST SCHOLAR.

My father slain! Serlsby, ward that.

The two Scholars *stab one another.*

59. father's is the abuse] *Q1–2*; father is abuse *Q3*.

60. father harm] *Q1*; father have harm *Q2–3*.

65. so] *Q1–2*; *not in Q3*.

66. this] *Q1–2*; thus *Q3*.

---

60. *harm*] (used intransitively) be harmed.
63. *event*] issue, outcome.
64. *Doubt'st . . . life*] do you fear for your life.
65. *A veney*] a fencing term; a bout (from Fr. *venue*, come on).
68. *ward*] guard.

2ND SCHOLAR.

And so is mine. Lambert, I'll quite thee well.

BUNGAY.

Oh, strange stratagem.

BACON.

See, friar, where the fathers both lie dead.
Bacon, thy magic doth effect this massacre.
This glass prospective worketh many woes;
And therefore, seeing these brave, lusty brutes,
These friendly youths did perish by thine art,
End all thy magic and thine art at once.
The poniard that did end the fatal lives
Shall break the cause efficiat of their woes.
So fade the glass, and end with it the shows
That nigromancy did infuse the crystal with.

He breaks the glass.

BUNGAY.

What means learned Bacon thus to break his glass?

BACON.

I tell thee, Bungay, it repents me sore
That ever Bacon meddled in this art.
The hours I have spent in pyromantic spells,
The fearful tossing in the latest night
Of papers full of nigromantic charms,
Conjuring and adjuring devils and fiends,
With stole and albe and strange pentaganon,
The wresting of the holy name of God,
As Sother, Eloim, and Adonai,

76. worketh] *Q1–2*; works *Q3*. 77. brave] *Q1*; *not in Q2–3*.
81. woes] *Q1–2*; vowes *Q3*. 93. Eloim] *Q2–3*; Elaim *Q1*.

---

73. *stratagem*] outcome, usually violent.
80. *fatal*] fated. 81. *cause efficiat*] cause effecting.
82. *shows*] visions, images.
91. *stole and albe*] sacred vestments.
92. *wresting*] misusing.
93–94. *Sother . . . Tetragrammaton*] various translations, substitutions, and emblematic words for the Hebrew word for "our Lord"; the original pronunciation of the Tetragrammaton is now thought to be represented in English by "Yahweh." The words (sometimes as anagrams) were thought to have occult powers in themselves.

Alpha, Manoth, and Tetragrammaton,
With praying to the five-fold powers of heaven,
Are instances that Bacon must be damn'd
For using devils to countervail his God.
Yet, Bacon, cheer thee; drown not in despair.
Sins have their salves. Repentance can do much.
Think Mercy sits where Justice holds her seat,
And from those wounds those bloody Jews did pierce,
Which by thy magic oft did bleed afresh,
From thence for thee the dew of mercy drops
To wash the wrath of high Jehovah's ire,
And make thee as a new-born babe from sin.
Bungay, I'll spend the remnant of my life
In pure devotion, praying to my God
That he would save what Bacon vainly lost.

Exit [*with* Bungay].

[xiv]

Enter Margaret *in nun's apparel;* Keeper, *her father; and their* friend.

KEEPER.

Margaret, be not so headstrong in these vows.
Oh, bury not such beauty in a cell,
That England hath held famous for the hue.
Thy father's hair, like to the silver blooms
That beautify the shrubs of Africa,
Shall fall before the dated time of death,
Thus to forgo his lovely Margaret.

MARGARET.

Ah, father, when the harmony of heaven
Soundeth the measures of a lively faith,

97. using] *Q1–2*; rising *Q3*.
97. his] *Q1–2*; with *Q3*.

[Scene xiv]
5. beautify] *Q1*; beautifies *Q2–3*.

95. *five-fold powers of heaven*] in reference to the five-pointed Pentagonon, at each point of which would be written a name of God.

102. *Which . . . bleed afresh*] i.e., which, because of magical abuses, bleed afresh in pain and grief for your sins.

[Scene xiv]

9. *measures*] harmony, musical beat.

9. *lively*] energetic, forceful.

The vain illusions of this flattering world
Seems odious to the thoughts of Margaret.
I loved once; Lord Lacy was my love;
And now I hate myself for that I lov'd,
And doted more on him than on my God.
For this, I scourge myself with sharp repents.
But now, the touch of such aspiring sins
Tells me all love is lust but love of heavens,
That beauty us'd for love is vanity.
The world contains naught but alluring baits,
Pride, flattery, and inconstant thoughts.
To shun the pricks of death I leave the world,
And vow to meditate on heavenly bliss,
To live in Framingham a holy nun,
Holy and pure in conscience and in deed;
And for to wish all maids to learn of me
To seek heaven's joy before earth's vanity.

FRIEND.

And will you then, Margaret, be shorn a nun, and so leave us all?

MARGARET.

Now, farewell, world, the engine of all woe.
Farewell to friends and father; welcome, Christ.
Adieu to dainty robes; this base attire
Better befits an humble mind to God
Than all the show of rich 'abiliments.
Love, oh love, and, with fond love, farewell,
Sweet Lacy, whom I loved once so dear;
Ever be well, but never in my thoughts,
Lest I offend to think on Lacy's love.
But even to that, as to the rest, farewell.

Enter Lacy, Warren, Ermsby, *booted and spurred.*

LACY.

Come on, my wags, we're near the keeper's lodge.

11. Seems] *Q1*; Seem *Q2–3*.

15. *repents*] penances.

29. *engine*] instrument.

Here have I oft walk'd in the wat'ry meads,
And chatted with my lovely Margaret.

WARREN.

Sirrah Ned, is not this the keeper?

LACY.

'Tis the same.

ERMSBY

The old lecher hath gotten holy mutton to him. A nun, my lord.

LACY.

Keeper, how farest thou? Holla, man, what cheer?
How doth Peggy, thy daughter and my love?

KEEPER.

Ah, good my lord, oh, woe is me for Peg!
See where she stands, clad in her nun's attire,
Ready for to be shorn in Framingham.
She leaves the world because she left your love.
Oh, good my lord, persuade her if you can.

LACY.

Why, how now, Margaret; what, a malcontent?
A nun? What holy father taught you this,
To task yourself to such a tedious life
As die a maid? 'Twere injury to me
To smother up such beauty in a cell.

MARGARET.

Lord Lacy, thinking of thy former 'miss,
How fond the prime of wanton years were spent
In love—oh, fie upon that fond conceit,
Whose hap and essence hangeth in the eye—
I leave both love and love's content at once,
Betaking me to Him that is true love,
And leaving all the world for love of Him.

48. Peg] *Q1–2*; Peggie *Q3*. 61. hap] *Q1–2*; hope *Q3*.

44. *mutton*] cant word for prostitute.
53. *malcontent*] one given over to melancholy.
55. *task yourself*] betake, apply.
58. *'miss*] amiss, error. 59. *fond*] foolishly.
61. *Whose hap . . . eye*] whose occasion and very nature are superficial.

LACY.
Whence, Peggy, comes this metamorphosis?
What, shorn a nun? And I have from the court
Posted with coursers to convey thee hence
To Windsor, where our marriage shall be kept.
Thy wedding robes are in the tailors' hands.
Come, Peggy, leave these peremptory vows.

MARGARET.
Did not my lord resign his interest,
And make divorce 'twixt Margaret and him?

LACY.
'Twas but to try sweet Peggy's constancy.
But will fair Margaret leave her love and lord?

MARGARET.
Is not heaven's joy before earth's fading bliss,
And life above sweeter than life in love?

LACY.
Why, then Margaret will be shorn a nun?

MARGARET.
Margaret hath made a vow which may not be revok'd.

WARREN.
We cannot stay, my lord; and if she be so strict,
Our leisure grants us not to woo afresh.

ERMSBY.
Choose you, fair damsel; yet the choice is yours.
Either a solemn nunnery or the court;
God or Lord Lacy. Which contents you best,
To be a nun, or else Lord Lacy's wife?

LACY.
A good motion. Peggy, your answer must be short.

MARGARET
The flesh is frail. My lord doth know it well,
That when he comes with his enchanting face,
Whatso'er betide, I cannot say him nay.

65. this] *Q1–2*; the *Q3*.
72. make] *Q1–2*; made *Q3*.
75. fading] *Q1–2*; *not in Q3*.

---

70. *peremptory*] absolute, unequivocal.
85. *a good motion*] i.e., a good way to put it.

Off goes the habit of a maiden's heart;
And, seeing Fortune will, fair Framingham,
And all the show of holy nuns, farewell.
Lacy for me, if he will be my lord.

LACY.

Peggy, thy lord, thy love, thy husband.
Trust me, by truth of knighthood, that the king
Stays for to marry matchless Eleanor
Until I bring thee richly to the court,
That one day may both marry her and thee.
How sayst thou, keeper? Art thou glad of this?

KEEPER.

As if the English king had given
The park and deer of Fressingfield to me.

ERMSBY.

I pray thee, my Lord of Sussex, why art thou in a brown study?

WARREN.

To see the nature of women, that be they never so near God, yet they love to die in a man's arms.

LACY.

What have you fit for breakfast? We have hied
And posted all this night to Fressingfield.

MARGARET.

Butter and cheese and humbles of a deer,
Such as poor keepers have within their lodge.

LACY.

And not a bottle of wine?

MARGARET.

We'll find one for my lord.

LACY.

Come, Sussex, let's in; we shall have more,
For she speaks least to hold her promise sure. *Exeunt.*

105–106.] *Collier; Q1–3 print as prose.*

111–112.] *Collier; Q1–3 print as prose.*

101–102. *brown study*] state of preoccupation, thoughtfulness.

107. *humbles*] entrails (liver, kidneys, heart).

112. *she speaks . . . sure*] i.e., she promises little so as to be able to fulfill what she speaks.

[xv] *Enter a* devil *to seek Miles.*

DEVIL.

How restless are the ghosts of hellish spirits
When every charmer with his magic spells
Calls us from nine-fold trenched Phlegiton,
To scud and over-scour the earth in post
Upon the speedy wings of swiftest winds.
Now Bacon hath rais'd me from the darkest deep
To search about the world for Miles his man,
For Miles, and to torment his lazy bones
For careless watching of his brazen head.
See where he comes. Oh, he is mine.

Enter Miles *with a gown and a cornercap.*

MILES.

A scholar, quoth you? Marry, sir, I would I had been made a bottle maker when I was made a scholar; for I can get neither to be a deacon, reader, nor schoolmaster; no, not the clerk of a parish. Some call me dunce; another saith my head is as full of Latin as an egg's full of oatmeal. Thus I am tormented that the devil and Friar Bacon haunts me. Good Lord, here's one of my master's devils. I'll go speak to him. What, Master Plutus, how cheer you?

DEVIL.

Dost thou know me?

MILES.

Know you, sir? Why, are not you one of my master's devils that were wont to come to my master, Doctor Bacon, at Brazen-nose?

1. spirits] *Q1*; sprites *Q2–3*.

3. Phlegiton] *Q2*; Blegiton *Q1*; Philegiton *Q3*.

---

2. *charmer*] wizard, magician.
3. *Phlegiton*] Phlegethon, a river of fire in Hades.
4. *scud*] hurry.
4. *over-scour*] search or sweep through or over.
10.1. *with a gown and a cornercap*] i.e., in academic dress.
18. *Plutus*] the god of wealth; Miles (or Greene) may have been thinking of Pluto, god of the underworld.

DEVIL.

Yes, marry, am I.

MILES.

Good Lord, Master Plutus, I have seen you a thousand times at my master's, and yet I had never the manners to make you drink. But, sir, I am glad to see how conformable you are to the statute. I warrant you he's as yeomanly a man as you shall see; mark you, masters, here's a plain, honest man, without welt or guard. But I pray you, sir, do you come lately from hell?

DEVIL.

Ay, marry; how then?

MILES.

Faith, 'tis a place I have desired long to see. Have you not good tippling houses there? May not a man have a lusty fire there, a pot of good ale, a pair of cards, a swinging piece of chalk, and a brown toast that will clap a white waistcoat on a cup of good drink?

DEVIL.

All this you may have there.

MILES.

You are for me, friend, and I am for you. But I pray you, may I not have an office there?

DEVIL.

Yes, a thousand. What wouldst thou be?

MILES.

By my troth, sir, in a place where I may profit myself. I

27–28. conformable] *Q1–2*; comfortabl *Q3*.
28. statute] *Q1*; state *Q2–3*.

---

28. *statute*] referring to one of many sumptuary laws restricting elaborate dress in certain professions or classes.

29. *mark you, masters*] addressed to the audience.

30. *welt . . . guard*] kinds of gold or silver lace facings for gowns; perhaps the quip is based on the devil's costume, which may have been skin-tight.

35. *pair*] pack.

35–36. *swinging*] large (slang).

36. *chalk*] used to add up accounts in alehouses.

37. *white waistcoat*] what we would call a head, or foam.

know hell is a hot place, and men are marvelous dry, and much drink is spent there. I would be a tapster.

DEVIL.

Thou shalt.

MILES.

There's nothing lets me from going with you, but that 'tis a long journey, and I have never a horse.

DEVIL.

Thou shalt ride on my back.

MILES.

Now surely here's a courteous devil, that for to pleasure his friend will not stick to make a jade of himself. But I pray you, goodman friend, let me move a question to you.

DEVIL.

What's that?

MILES.

I pray you, whether is your pace a trot or an amble?

DEVIL.

An amble.

MILES.

'Tis well. But take heed it be not a trot. But 'tis no matter; I'll prevent it.

DEVIL.

What dost?

MILES.

Marry, friend, I put on my spurs; for if I find your pace either a trot or else uneasy, I'll put you to a false gallop; I'll make you feel the benefit of my spurs.

DEVIL.

Get up upon my back.

MILES.

Oh, Lord, here's even a goodly marvel, when a man rides to hell on the devil's back. *Exeunt roaring.*

---

46. *lets*] prevents, hinders.
50. *stick*] stand upon terms, scruple.
60. *false gallop*] a jerky trot.

[xvi]

Enter the Emperor *with a pointless sword; next, the* King of Castile, *carrying a sword with a point;* Lacy, *carrying the globe;* Ed[ward]; Warr[en], *carrying a rod of gold with a dove on it;* Ermsby, *with a crown and scepter;* [Princess Eleanor], *with the* Fair Maid of Fressingfield *on her left hand;* Henry, Bacon, *with other Lords attending.*

EDWARD.

Great potentates, earth's miracles for state,
Think that Prince Edward humbles at your feet,
And, for these favors, on his martial sword
He vows perpetual homage to yourselves,
Yielding these honors unto Eleanor.

HENRY.

Gramercies, lordlings. Old Plantagenet,
That rules and sways the Albion diadem,
With tears discovers these conceived joys,
And vows requital, if his men-at-arms,
The wealth of England, or due honors done
To Eleanor, may quite his favorites.
But all this while, what say you to the dames,
That shine like to the crystal lamps of heaven?

EMPEROR.

If but a third were added to these two,
They did surpass those gorgeous images
That gloried Ida with rich beauty's wealth.

MARGARET.

'Tis I, my lords, who humbly on my knee

0.4. *Princess Eleanor*] *Collier; The queene Q1–3.*

6. lordlings] *Q1*; lordings *Q2–3.*

16. beauty's] *Q1–2*; beauteous *Q3.*

0.1. *pointless sword*] the blunted sword of Edward the Confessor, signifying mercy.

0.2. *sword with a point*] signifying justice. 0.2. *globe*] the royal orb.

0.3. *rod of gold . . . dove on it*] a type of scepter signifying equity; the dove represents the sanctifying power of the Holy Ghost.

2. *humbles*] humbles himself, kneels.

15–16. *They . . . beauty's wealth*] i.e., they would surpass the beauties of Juno, Pallas, and Venus, the goddesses who, on Mt. Ida, commanded Paris to judge who was most beautiful.

Must yield her orisons to mighty Jove,
For lifting up his handmaid to this state,
Brought from her homely cottage to the court,
And grac'd with kings, princes, and emperors;
To whom, next to the noble Lincoln earl,
I vow obedience and such humble love
As may a handmaid to such mighty men.

ELEANOR.

Thou martial man that wears the Almain crown,
And you the western potentates of might,
The Albion princess, English Edward's wife,
Proud that the lovely star of Fressingfield,
Fair Margaret, countess to the Lincoln earl,
Attends on Eleanor—gramercies, lord, for her—
'Tis I give thanks for Margaret to you all,
And rest, for her, due bounden to yourselves.

HENRY.

Seeing the marriage is solemnized,
Let's march in triumph to the royal feast.
But why stands Friar Bacon here so mute?

BACON.

Repentant for the follies of my youth,
That magic's secret mysteries misled,
And joyful that this royal marriage
Portends such bliss unto this matchless realm.

HENRY.

Why, Bacon, what strange event shall happen to this land?
Or what shall grow from Edward and his queen?

BACON.

I find by deep prescience of mine art,
Which once I temper'd in my secret cell,

18. Jove] *Q1–2*; love *Q3*.

---

20. *homely*] humble.

42–62. Bacon's prognostication should be compared to Cranmer's great glorification of Queen Elizabeth in Shakespeare's *Henry VIII,* V.v.15–64.

That here where Brute did build his Troynovant,
From forth the royal garden of a king
Shall flourish out so rich and fair a bud
Whose brightness shall deface proud Phoebus' flower,
And over-shadow Albion with her leaves.
Till then Mars shall be master of the field;
But then the stormy threats of wars shall cease.
The horse shall stamp as careless of the pike;
Drums shall be turn'd to timbrels of delight;
With wealthy favors plenty shall enrich
The strond that gladded wand'ring Brute to see,
And peace from heaven shall harbor in these leaves
That gorgeous beautifies this matchless flower.
Apollo's hellitropian then shall stoop,
And Venus' hyacinth shall vail her top;
Juno shall shut her gilliflowers up,
And Pallas' bay shall bash her brightest green;
Ceres' carnation, in consort with those,
Shall stoop and wonder at Diana's rose.

HENRY.

This prophecy is mystical.
But, glorious commanders of Europa's love,
That makes fair England like that wealthy isle
Circled with Gihon and swift Euphrates,

48. leaves] *Q1–2*; loves *Q3*. 66. swift] *Dyce 2*; first *Q1–3*.

---

44. *Brute . . . Troynovant*] referring to the pseudo-historical legend that the great-grandson of Aeneas, called Brute (or Brut), sailed from Italy to England and founded London, which he named New Troy, or Troynovant, thus making Englishmen the descendants of the Trojans.

47. *Phoebus' flower*] the sunflower.

51. *careless*] fearless. 54. *gladded*] caused to rejoice.

57. *hellitropian*] heliotrope, sunflower.

58. *vail*] doff, lower. 60. *bash*] doff, in humility (see ii.151).

61. *in consort*] in harmony, accompanying.

62. *Diana's rose*] i.e., the Tudor rose of the Virgin queen.

63. *mystical*] allegorical, expressed in figures.

65. *That makes*] who make.

65–66. *that wealthy isle . . . Euphrates*] cf. Shakespeare's *Richard II*, II.i.42, "This other Eden, demi-paradise."

66. *Gihon*] the "name of the second river" flowing out of Eden, Genesis ii:13.

In royalizing Henry's Albion
With presence of your princely mightiness,
Let's march. The tables all are spread,
And viands such as England's wealth affords
Are ready set to furnish out the boards.
You shall have welcome, mighty potentates;
It rests to furnish up this royal feast.
Only your hearts be frolic, for the time
Craves that we taste of naught but jouissance.
Thus glories England over all the west. *Exeunt omnes.*

Finis Friar Bacon, made by Robert Greene,
Master of Arts.
Omne tulit punctum qui miscuit utile dulci.

74. be] *Q1–2*; are *Q3*. 76.1–2. *Finis . . . Arts*] *Q1*; *not in Q2–3*

---

73. *rests*] remains.
75. *jouissance*] joy, pleasure.
76.3. *Omne . . . dulci*] "He will win everybody's vote who blends what is instructive with what is delightful"; Greene's favorite motto, from Horace *Ars Poetica* 343.

Appendix A

Note to Stage Direction beginning Scene xi

This is the most troublesome stage direction in the play.[1] If we understood it, we should know much more about an inner acting area, or "inner stage" (if there was one), in the Tudor public theaters. We should also be able to draw one or two conclusions regarding the style of movement on this stage; the placement of actors and properties on such a stage is an important factor in determining whether Elizabethan acting was highly "formal" (from a modern point of view) or realistically oriented. The phrase, "drawing the curtains," is important. At line 37, Bacon finishes his long speech with "Draw close the curtains, Miles. Now, for thy life,/ Be watchful, and—" —falling asleep on the last words.

Are we to assume that Bacon wants the brazen head hidden? This is hardly possible, since he orders Miles to watch it, and the following portion of the scene demands the head in full view. Which curtains, then, does Bacon wish drawn "close"? If Bacon falls asleep in the "inner stage" (using the term for convenience, since every reader will know approximately the acting area intended), and if Miles closes these curtains before him—presumably, the same curtains Bacon opened on his entrance—then the head and the other properties must have been moved, in the meantime, to the main acting area, downstage on the large projecting apron. There is a stage direction in Greene's *Alphonsus* which has always been taken as an indication of the position of the head in *Friar Bacon*: "*Let there be a brazen Head set in the middle of the place behind the Stage, out of which, cast flames of*

[1] The reader is referred to Professor Richard Hosley's forthcoming book, *Elizabethan Playhouse Stages: A Study of Theatrical Form in the Age of Shakespeare*; Hosley's discussions, in recent articles, of the "discovery space" in the Tudor stages are carefully documented and set forth with good common sense.

fire, drums rumble within, Enter two Priests" (ll. 1245–1247). If the head in our play is "in the middle of the place behind the Stage," we can be fairly sure that this is not as well the place in which Bacon falls asleep; and, unless we postulate a bed or structural bedroom with curtains of some kind on the main acting area, downstage, this does indeed seem to be the place in which he does so. Unhappily, there are further possibilities which complicate the problem. For example, Bacon may have delivered all or part of the long speech (ll. 7–38) from an acting area above, and fallen asleep there. If so, was Miles supposed to follow him up, and close the curtains there? This is hardly likely, for we may be fairly sure that stage business which is cumbersome in description will be equally so in actual stage performance. If Friar Bacon, then, sleeps in the same place in which he makes his entrance, and from which he is to emerge again at line 80, where is the brazen head?

There is really no reason why the head in *Friar Bacon* must be in precisely the same place on stage as the head in *Alphonsus*. Perhaps this property was in approximately the same place as the apple tree and dragon conjured up by Bungay (ix.83.1–2)—that is, over the trap door, on the main apron. This would make for convenience in the destruction of the head—but would increase the difficulty in explaining the "hand" which appears, "that breaketh down the Head with a hammer." At this point, all ingenious solutions should be distrusted, for in a combination of circumstances which make staging appear very complicated, it is most likely that in fact the solution was quite simple.

It is now generally agreed that the area which for convenience we have called an "inner stage" did not exist in the public theater —at least, not in the terms in which scholars at one time imagined it. Perhaps this space was more in the nature of an "entrance area"—that is, large enough to provide for important "discoveries" (e.g., *2 Tamburlaine*, S.D. at l. 2968: "*The Arras is drawen, and Zenocrate lies in her bed of state, Tamburlaine sitting by her: three Phisitians about her bed, tempering potions. Theridamas, Techelles, Vsumcasane, and the three sonnes*"—eleven persons, some of them involved in stage business; some properties; and a large structure, the "bed of state"), but intended to serve also for a certain amount of acting which was not to remain in that area for more than a few minutes. For example, in the tableau of Zenocrate's death, the actors did not, in all probability, maintain the initial stage "picture," and, except for Zenocrate, may have moved downstage after "the Arras [was] drawen." Since such a large proportion of any audience in the public theaters would have seen the stage from above, from the surrounding galleries of the theater, any group of actors on stage would have had to consider the important question of sight-lines to the apron; and any inner area would have been at least partly obscured by the overhanging "Heavens," or stage roof—even though this protruded at some height above the floor.

Friar Bacon's entrance is accompanied by many properties, including the head. Perhaps he was to draw the curtains—that is, as in the *2 Tamburlaine* stage direction, to *open* them—and then simply walked downstage on the main apron. If Miles entered with the properties (a logical means to have them moved into the acting area), he probably did the same thing. If the head had to be placed over the trap door, either Bacon or Miles could move it during the long speech, as a normal piece of supporting stage business. If the head remained in the "entrance area" upstage, however, Bacon himself would not fall asleep far from it. This is the less likely solution, since it would deprive the actor playing Miles of some area in which to move during the comic sequence about to take place. If the head was placed just downstage of the discovery area, however, with Bacon sitting, then falling asleep, downstage-right or -left of center (perhaps against one of the columns, opposite the one upon which Miles is soon to "knock [his] head"), the head would remain visible (and accessible to the "hand . . . with a hammer" that is to destroy it), and Miles would have plenty of walking area for his part of the scene. The actual proximity of the actor playing Bacon to the noise and action upstage center would not have introduced a problem of verisimilitude (see note to S.D., vi.0.1).

Appendix B

Chronology

	Political and Literary Events	*Life and Major Works of Greene*
1558	Accession of Queen Elizabeth. Thomas Kyd born.	Robert Greene born at Norwich, July 11.
1560	George Chapman born.	
1561	Francis Bacon born.	
1564	Shakespeare born. Christopher Marlowe born.	
1570	Thomas Heywood born.*	
1572	Ben Jonson born. Thomas Dekker born.* John Donne born. Massacre of St. Bartholomew's Day.	
1573		Matriculates at Corpus Christi College, Cambridge (?).
1575		Enters St. John's College, Cambridge.
1576	The Theatre, the first permanent public theater in London, established by James Burbage. John Marston born.	

*Indicates that the year is approximate.
(?) Indicates that occurrence is in doubt.

1577	
The Curtain theater opened. Holinshed's *Chronicles of England, Scotland and Ireland.* Drake begins circumnavigation of the earth; completed 1580.	Travels to Italy (?).*
1578	
	Receives B.A., St. John's.
1579	
John Fletcher born. John Lyly's *Euphues: The Anatomy of Wit* published.	
1580	
Thomas Middleton born.	*Mamillia,* Part One.
1583	
Philip Massinger born.	Receives Cambridge M.A. *Mamillia,* Part Two.
1584	
Francis Beaumont born.*	*Card of Fancy.*
1585	
	Planetomachia. Calls himself a "Student of Phisicke." Returns to Norwich to marry (?).*
1586	
Death of Sir Philip Sidney. John Ford born.	Deserts wife and child, goes to London (?).* First associations with the players.*
1587	
The Rose theater opened by Henslowe. Marlowe's *TAMBURLAINE,* Part I.* Execution of Mary, Queen of Scots.	*Farewell to Folly.* *ALPHONSUS KING OF ARAGON.**
1588	
Defeat of the Spanish Armada. Marlowe's *TAMBURLAINE* Part II.*	Receives Oxford M.A. *Perimedes the Blacksmith.* *Pandosto.*

(?) Indicates that occurrence is in doubt.
*Indicates that the year is approximate.

1589

Marlowe's *THE JEW OF MALTA*.*

Kyd's *THE SPANISH TRAGEDY*.*

FRIAR BACON AND FRIAR BUNGAY.*

1590

Spenser's *Faerie Queene* (Books I–III) published.

Sidney's *Arcadia* published.

Shakespeare's *HENRY VI*, Parts I–III,* *TITUS ANDRONICUS*.*

*A LOOKING-GLASS FOR LONDON AND ENGLAND** (with Lodge).

GEORGE-A-GREENE (?).*

1591

Shakespeare's *RICHARD III*.*

First and second parts of *Conny-catching*.

ORLANDO FURIOSO.*

JAMES THE FOURTH.*

1592

Marlowe's *DOCTOR FAUSTUS** and *EDWARD II*.*

Shakespeare's *TAMING OF THE SHREW** and *THE COMEDY OF ERRORS*.*

A Quip for an Upstart Courtier.

Greene's Groatsworth of Wit, in which appears an attack on Shakespeare.

Greene dies, poverty-stricken in London, September 2 or 3.

The Repentance of Robert Greene (posthumous).

1593

Shakespeare's *LOVE'S LABOUR'S LOST*;* *Venus and Adonis* published.

Death of Marlowe.

Theaters closed on account of plague.

1594

Shakespeare's *TWO GENTLEMEN OF VERONA*;* *The Rape of Lucrece* published.

Shakespeare's company becomes Lord Chamberlain's Men.

James Shirley born.*

Death of Kyd.

(?) Indicates that occurrence is in doubt.
*Indicates that the year is approximate.

1595

The Swan theater built.

Sidney's *Defense of Poesy* published.

Shakespeare's *ROMEO AND JULIET,* A MIDSUMMER NIGHT'S DREAM,* RICHARD II.**

Raleigh's first expedition to Guiana.

1596

Spenser's *Faerie Queene* (Books IV–VI) published.

Shakespeare's *MERCHANT OF VENICE,* KING JOHN.**

1597

Bacon's *Essays* (first edition).

Shakespeare's *HENRY IV,* Part I.*

1598

Demolition of the Theatre.

Shakespeare's *MUCH ADO ABOUT NOTHING,* HENRY IV,* Part II.*

Jonson's *EVERY MAN IN HIS HUMOR* (first version).

Seven books of Chapman's translation of Homer's *Iliad* published.

1599

The Globe theater opened.

Shakespeare's *AS YOU LIKE IT,* HENRY V,* JULIUS CAESAR.**

Dekker's *THE SHOEMAKERS' HOLIDAY.**

Death of Spenser.

1600

Shakespeare's *TWELFTH NIGHT,* HAMLET.**

Marston's *ANTONIO AND MELLIDA,* ANTONIO'S REVENGE.**

The Fortune theater built by Alleyn.

*Indicates that the year is approximate.

Chronology

1601

Shakespeare's *MERRY WIVES OF WINDSOR.**

Insurrection and execution of the Earl of Essex.

1602

Shakespeare's *TROILUS AND CRESSIDA,* ALL'S WELL THAT ENDS WELL.**

1603

Death of Queen Elizabeth; accession of James VI of Scotland as James I.

Florio's translation of Montaigne's *Essays* published.

Heywood's *A WOMAN KILLED WITH KINDNESS.*

Marston's *THE MALCONTENT.**

Shakespeare's company becomes the King's Men.

1604

Shakespeare's *MEASURE FOR MEASURE,* OTHELLO.**

Marston's *THE FAWN.**

Chapman's *BUSSY D'AMBOIS.**

1605

Shakespeare's *KING LEAR.**

Marston's *THE DUTCH COURTEZAN.**

Bacon's *Advancement of Learning* published.

The Gunpowder Plot.

1606

Shakespeare's *MACBETH.**

Jonson's *VOLPONE.**

Tourneur's *REVENGER'S TRAGEDY.**

The Red Bull theater built.

1607

Shakespeare's *ANTONY AND CLEOPATRA.**

*Indicates that the year is approximate.

Beaumont's *KNIGHT OF THE BURNING PESTLE.**
Settlement of Jamestown, Virginia.

1608
Shakespeare's *CORIOLANUS,* TIMON OF ATHENS,* PERICLES.**
Chapman's *CONSPIRACY AND TRAGEDY OF CHARLES, DUKE OF BYRON.**
Richard Burbage leases Blackfriars Theatre for King's Company.
John Milton born.

1609
Shakespeare's *CYMBELINE;** *Sonnets* published.
Jonson's *EPICOENE.*

1610
Jonson's *ALCHEMIST.*
Chapman's *REVENGE OF BUSSY D'AMBOIS.**

1611
Authorized (King James) Version of the Bible published.
Shakespeare's *THE WINTER'S TALE,* THE TEMPEST.**
Beaumont and Fletcher's *A KING AND NO KING.*
Tourneur's *ATHEIST'S TRAGEDY.**

1612
Webster's *THE WHITE DEVIL.**

1613
The Globe theater burned.
Shakespeare's *HENRY VIII* (with Fletcher).
Webster's *THE DUCHESS OF MALFI.**
Middleton's *A CHASTE MAID IN CHEAPSIDE.*

*Indicates that the year is approximate.